Cape Cod

Its Natural and Cultural History
By Robert Finch

D0035648

A Guide to Cape Cod
National Seashore
Massachusetts

Produced by the
Division of Publications
National Park Service

U.S. Department of the Interior
Washington, D.C.

Using This Handbook
The Cape Cod peninsula extending into the Atlantic
Ocean off Massachusetts is one of America's prime
coastal recreational areas. Cape Cod National Seashore, managed by the National Park Service, ex-
tends for 40 miles along the the Cape's outer arm
between Chatham and Provincetown. In Part 1 of
this handbook, author and longtime resident Robert
Finch introduces the reader to the Cape's rich
cultural and natural history and to the National
Seashore. In the three chapters of Part 2, Finch more
closely examines the land, the sea, and the transformations that have taken place in recent years. Picto-
rial features on various Cape aspects supplement
these chapters. Part 3 presents concise travel guide
and reference materials, including a full-color map.

National Park Handbooks are published to support
the National Park Service's management programs
and to promote understanding and enjoyment of the
more than 360 National Park System sites. Each
handbook is intended to be informative reading and
a useful guide before, during, and after a park visit.
The handbooks are sold at parks and can be pur-
chased by mail from the Superintendent of Docu-
ments, U.S. Government Printing Office, Washington,
DC 20402-9325.

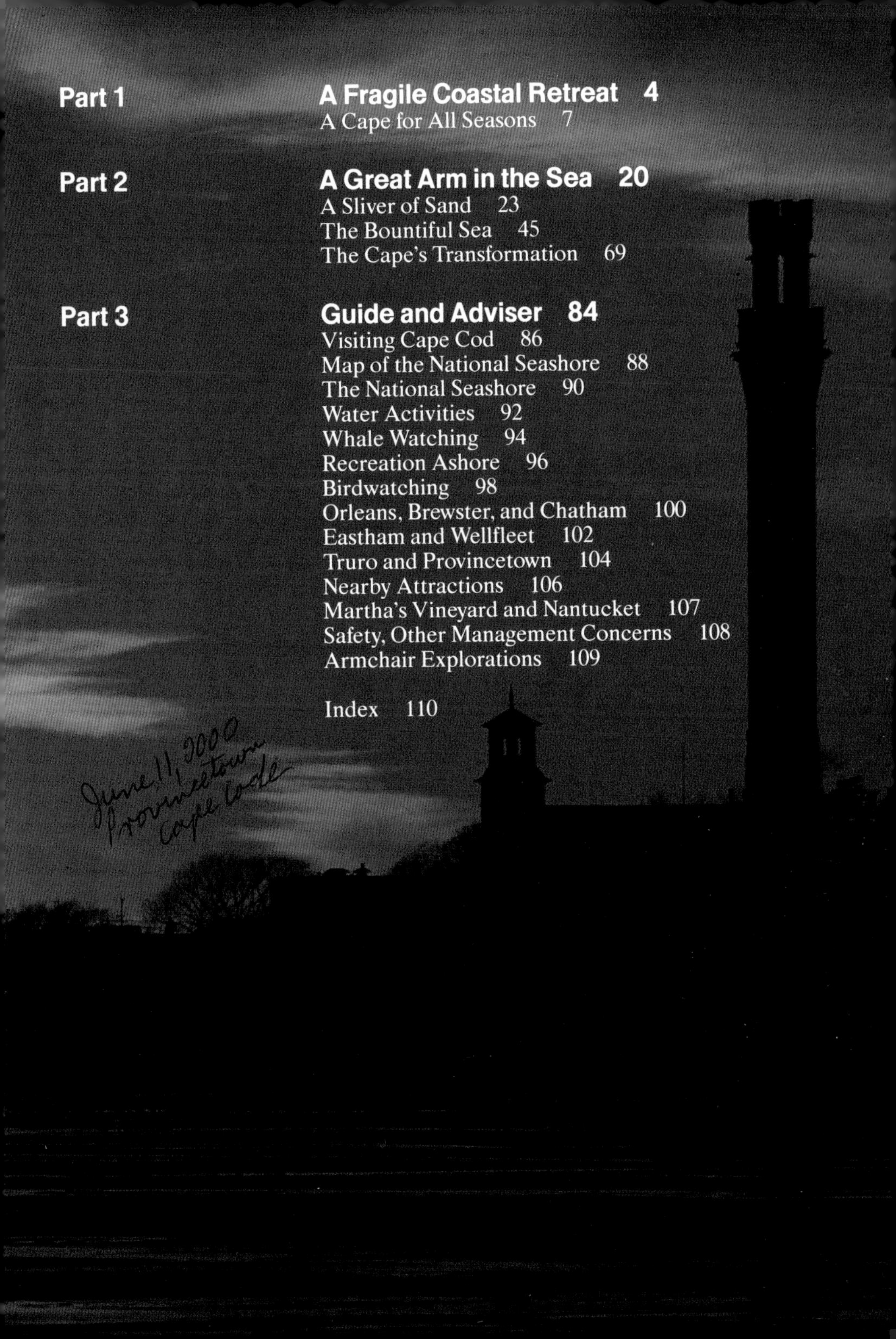

June 11, 2000
Provincetown
Cape Code

Part 1

A Fragile Coastal Retreat

A Cape for All Seasons

Majestically eroded, the great glacial bluffs of Cape Cod's outer beach rise from the open Atlantic, separating the ocean from Cape Cod Bay. Its many-colored sands and clays flow grain by grain, or in sudden shelving slabs, to replenish the shore below. The beach, broad and gently sloping in summer, short and steep in winter, arcs northward for more than 20 miles, giving the walker a curved prospect two or three miles ahead at most. And always, coming onto the shore and reforming it, with measured cadences in calm weather, with awesome fury during northeast gales, is the sea. Here, as Henry Beston put it, "the ocean encounters the last defiant bulwark of two worlds." There is no other landscape like it anywhere.

Cape Cod holds a special place in America's landscape, history, and collective imagination. As the world's largest glacial peninsula, it juts farther out into the Atlantic Ocean than any other part of the United States. It was one of the earliest landfalls of the European explorers in the 16th and 17th centuries. Its purported identity as the "Wonderstrand" of the Viking sagas remains apocryphal, but it was—as every Cape Codder will be quick to tell you—indisputably the *first* landing place of the *Mayflower* Pilgrims in 1620, and it became one of the oldest settled areas in the country.

Cape Codders early on took to the sea with a will, and they have never relinquished it. Over the centuries there developed on this thin peninsula a unique maritime way of life that has produced some of the most familiar objects and images in American culture. They include that durable architectural form, the Cape Cod house; indigenous nautical designs such as the Cape Cod catboat; tools like the quahog bullrake; and such functional folk art as carved bird decoys. Cape Cod bogs produced the first commercial cranberries, that traditional part of our Thanksgiving celebrations. The Cape's villages, low hills,

7

Fishermen's floats, weathered-shingled boathouses, and cat-boats—Cape Cod's coves reflect its seafaring traditions.

Pages 10-11: *Because the Outer Cape is such a narrow strip of land with the Atlantic on one side and Cape Cod Bay on the other, sunrises and sunsets can be spectacular. Here the sun rises over Eastham's Nauset Marsh, which was a harbor when Champlain explored the area in 1606.*

and sandy shores are still dotted with gray shingled windmills, looking like ungainly landbound ships, whose great sheeted arms once ground corn and pumped seawater for the making of salt; tall lighthouses that stand sentry on bold eroding sea cliffs and at the entrances to low, protected harbors; stately sea captains' houses with roofs crowned with "widows walks" and yard gates framed by arched whale jaws; and, from local wharves and piers, fleets of colorful boats manned by fishermen who continue to go out to harvest the sea as they have for centuries.

Perhaps the most enduring image of all, however, is that of the legendary "Cape Codder" himself. He appears in many guises: as a Portuguese "banker" fisherman trawling for cod in a small dory off the Georges Banks; a Truro "mooncusser" salvaging the booty from an 18th-century pirate ship wrecked on the Cape's "backside;" a Wampanoag Indian gathering alewives, or migratory herring, in spring to plant with her corn; a Wellfleet whaler casting his harpoon at a right whale in the icy Arctic seas; a Yankee clipper ship skipper from Brewster or Dennis helping to open up the China Trade or setting a transoceanic sailing record that still stands today; a Cape Verdean girl picking ripe wine-colored cranberries in the long rows of a Harwich bog; a Chatham Life Saving Serviceman pulling his surfboat through a fierce January gale to make a daring rescue of the crew of a vessel grounded on one of the Cape's treacherous shoals; a Provincetown rum-runner in his weather-beaten dragger eluding a Coast Guard cutter in the fog; an "old salt" in sou'wester and knee boots spinning yarns in Barnstable or Rock Harbor.

These and other versions of the protean Cape Codder have been celebrated and recorded in story and song since the founding of this country and have become a part of our history and folklore. In fact, few if any rural areas of comparable size have been written, painted, and sung about so richly over the years as the Cape landscape and its inhabitants.

Still, the dominant image of Cape Cod for most Americans today is probably that of one of the Nation's most popular summer playgrounds. For two centuries countless visitors and vacationers have escaped the burdens and the routines of daily life for a day, a week, or a season of liberation, exploration, relaxation, and recreation along the Cape's

unsurpassed beaches, ponds, marshes, bays, pine barrens, inlets, and dunes. Originally a summer resort for Bostonians and other New Englanders, the Cape now receives visitors from everywhere, at all seasons of the year. One of the favorite summer games for Cape children is to see how many different state license plates they can spot. Not infrequently they can get them all, including Alaska and Hawaii—as well as the Canadian provinces, Mexico, and several European countries. Where Cape Cod once produced seamen who sailed around the globe to bring home wealth and exotic treasures, the Cape has in turn become host to much of the world, providing the setting for countless beach parties, clambakes, family outings, sailing and fishing trips, summer romances, and increasingly, an appreciation and enjoyment of its rich environment, history, and natural resources.

Gulls seem to be everywhere, but the variety of birds makes Cape Cod a birdwatcher's paradise throughout the year. Along shorelines, tides rhythmically polish shells and cobbles.

What constitutes the enduring allure of a place like Cape Cod? What makes more people than ever cross the Cape Cod Canal bridges at all seasons in search of something they believe lies in promise for them here despite ever-increasing traffic jams, crowded beaches, the continuing proliferation of honky-tonk tourist traps, and the ongoing fragmentation of woodlands and waterfronts by commercial and residential development?

Over the centuries the universal and nearly perfect image of Cape Cod as a flexed human arm has provided an ambivalent symbol for what its settlers and visitors have hoped to find here. For the fearful yet hopeful Pilgrim passengers on the *Mayflower* it both beckoned and threatened, offering religious liberty and land for settlement, yet at the same time presenting, in William Bradford's words, "a wild and savage hue," a "hideous and desolate wilderness" that many of them would not survive.

To their maritime descendants the Cape offered seemingly endless abundance from the sea and a springboard to personal fortune; yet at the same time it proved to be a treacherous barrier to sea traffic, a graveyard for hundreds of ships that fell victim to the Cape's treacherous rips and shoals, or to fierce northeast storms and gales. It was not by chance, or merely to escape the wind, that most old Cape houses are built well back from the shore. As Rowena Myers, an 88-year-old lifetime resident of

Winds and tides constantly move the sands, tearing down dunes and creating new ones.

Orleans once explained to me, "The old people didn't like to look at the sea once they were ashore. It held too much pain for them."

Today Cape Cod beckons as never before to a Nation increasingly starved, in Henry Beston's words, "for lack of elemental things, for fire before the hands, for water welling from the earth, for air, for the dear earth itself underfoot." Seventy-five million of us live within a day's drive of Barnstable County. During the past 30 years the Cape's permanent population has risen from 70,000 to 190,000, a figure that nearly triples during the peak summer season.

Some come to walk the spacious curved length of the Great Beach of Cape Cod, which Thoreau claimed was a place where "a man may stand and put all America behind him" (though at many public beaches in July and August it may seem as if one has most of America in front of him!). Others seek quieter places like the soft pine barrens of the interior woodlands, or one of the Cape's hundreds of clear kettle-hole ponds, or the dune country of the Province Lands with its eccentric and colorful community of dune shacks—an ever-shifting landscape of mirages and stark, unexpected beauty.

Still others find, along the Cape's many well-preserved village streets, in its old farmhouses and meandering stone walls of glacial boulders, its lighthouses, fishing shacks, and aging fleets of sea-beaten draggers and lobster boats, a deep sense of that earnest, abiding, communal history that flourished here for so long and which we seek to borrow to help anchor our more modern, shifting lives.

Many are attracted to the energetic and often outrageous bohemian diversity of a place like Provincetown, or to the Cape's many art galleries, theaters, concerts, and museums. Some may hope for a glimpse of the Kennedy compound in Hyannisport or a movie star on the bench in front of a local general store. Others look forward to a Cape Cod lobster and clam dinner (which may, in fact, have come from the waters off Maine or Alaska) at a waterfront restaurant, or the seemingly endless array of gift shops, night spots, and tourist diversions (including increasingly elaborate miniature golf courses with waterfalls and "historic reproductions")—much of which have little or no indigenous connection with Cape Cod and can be had elsewhere, but which somehow seem to mean more when experienced here.

One element that seems to embrace and permeate all of the Cape's attractions is natural change. Change, of course, takes place in any environment, but here on the Cape it seems peculiarly pervasive, visible, and dramatic, particularly along the ocean shore. I like to point out to people who want to retrace Thoreau's famous walk along the Outer Beach that they are likely to get pretty wet if they try it, since Thoreau's original path now lies several hundred feet offshore!

We are subject to great periodic sea changes on this peninsula. Tides rise and fall up to nine feet twice a day, sweeping out in places in Cape Cod Bay to reveal tidal flats over a mile in extent. Waves and currents continuously undermine and cut into the great glacial cliffs of the Outer Cape, removing an average of three feet a year from our eastern boundary. Autumn and winter storms rearrange the ocean beaches, undermining the foundations of lighthouses, beach parking lots, and shorefront cottages, strewing the beaches at times with the carcasses of thousands of sea creatures, from whelks to whales. Tides and winds build and unbuild ridges and bowls of sand dunes, which in turn march across the land, threatening to bury marshes, forests, ponds, roads, and, in the past, whole villages and harbors. Major storms, like that of the Great Blizzard of February 6-7, 1978, change the very outlines of Cape Cod, cutting barrier beaches in two, creating new islands, flattening entire dune systems, creating new inlets, and plugging up old ones. The Cape is a river of sand into which we can never step twice.

For whatever reasons we come, the continuing attraction of the Cape to tourists and new residents (known as "washashores") has proven a mixed blessing, providing a valuable source of income to the local populace but also bringing an increase in development and commercialization that threatens the very things we seek here: clean air, unpolluted waters and beaches, the harvest of the sea, unspoiled vistas, a sense of rooted historical continuity, the free interplay of natural forces and wild inhabitants, and the opportunity for discovery and self-discovery in a landscape that has had a perennial allure for the human spirit for over three and a half centuries.

In stark contrast with the sandy shorelines, the upper Herring River in Wellfleet is rich in vegetation.

It was with the intent of preserving this experience for the public at large, and not for just a privileged few, that the idea for the National Seashore was born more than 30 years ago. The formation of the National Seashore was unique among the creation of the Nation's public parks. Prior to its establishment in 1961, national parks, forests, seashores, and monuments had been created from land already owned by federal or state governments, or from land or funds donated by private individuals. No federal monies had ever been spent to create such places.

On August 7, 1961, when President John F. Kennedy signed the legislation establishing Cape Cod National Seashore, he declared: "I . . . hope that this will be one of a whole series of great seashore parks which will be for the inspiration and enjoyment of people all over the United States." Since then, others indeed have been created and Cape Cod National Seashore has become one of the most popular of the Nation's public parks, with more than five million visits each year. The diligent and dedicated participation of the Seashore's Advisory Commission, composed of 10 state, county, and town representatives, helped park officials devise the first comprehensive master plan for the National Seashore. Nonetheless, the "balancing act" of preservation, recreation, and local rights has not always been an easy or a smooth one. Debates continue over recreational demands versus conservation, controversial uses such as beach buggy access, and development within the park. But there are relatively few who do not recognize not only the economic importance of the Seashore but the critical role it has played in realizing former Senator Leverett Saltonstall's dream of maintaining Cape Cod "so that other Americans, in dire need of the natural grandeur of the clean, open spaces, will find an outlet from their crowded, grimy, urban lives."

What you will find here is a different experience from what is offered in our national parks and most of the other national seashores. There is stunning scenic beauty and wildlife in abundance, to be sure, and the chance to explore and enjoy them on foot, horseback, or bicycle, in a canoe or a sailboat, on a guided walk, at an interpretive talk, or, if you like, simply lying on a beach before the rolling waves.

But there is also, by design and intent, the ongoing

Today Nauset Light alerts mariners off Eastham's treacherous Atlantic coast. Since the days of the earliest Indian inhabitants, Cape Codders have plied the bay and ocean for food and related marine products. Commercial fishing boats still work out of Provincetown, Chatham, and Wellfleet within the National Seashore.

On a cloudy day, the Cape's most obvious icon, the codfish, keeps track of the wind. With a change in the weather, Nauset Marsh glows in autumn light.

presence of man, in the hundreds of historic houses, lighthouses, Coast Guard stations, and summer cottages that remain within the Seashore, and in the continuing traditional uses of its lands and waters, such as commercial fishing, lobstering and shellfishing, hunting and berry picking.

The boundaries between Seashore lands, private property, and community facilities are not always obvious. The Provincetown airport and the Nauset Regional High School in Eastham, for instance, both lie within Seashore boundaries. Visitors are asked to observe the "Private Property—Please Respect Owner's Rights" signs they encounter along many of the Seashore roads and trails. A number of the more popular beaches require local town parking stickers. Cape Cod National Seashore, in other words, is not so much a protected pristine preserve as an ongoing experiment in cooperation between the Federal Government and local communities and their residents who continue to live, work, and play alongside, and often within, the park itself.

Whether you choose to join the summer crowds, or seek a solitary walk along the winter beach, we hope this handbook will acquaint you with enough knowledge of Cape Cod's rich historic and natural heritage so that your visit here, whether brief or extended, will be more rewarding.

Part 2

A Great Arm in the Sea

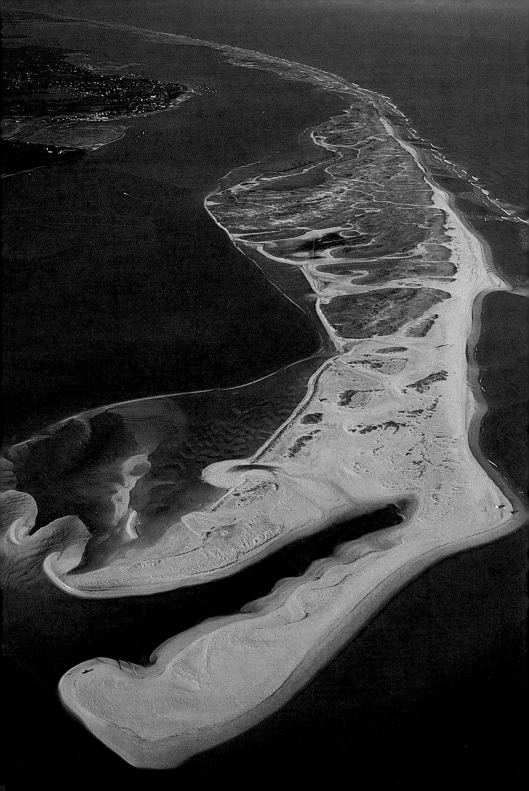

A Sliver of Sand

Overwashes of sand become readily apparent from the air over North Beach off Chatham.

Pages 20-21: *This satellite view clearly shows the flexed arm shape of the Cape.*

From the air the great curled arm of Cape Cod looks like a mere film of sand, a whimsical momentary shape floating on the vast ocean around it. Its flimsy fabric appears torn and rent by hundreds of holes, large and small, and dozens of slits at the edges, where the water shows through. So sheer and vulnerable does it appear that it seems as if the slightest push might sink it beneath the sea.

This somewhat fanciful impression nonetheless contains several grains of geologic truth, for water, in its various guises, permeates the Cape's past, present, and future. Created by the frozen water of vast glaciers, shaped today by the water of tides, waves, currents, and storm surges, this prominent hook of land is destined to succumb at last to the steadily rising waters of the sea—all in the merest flick of geologic time.

Some 75,000 years ago, when the Earth's climate entered a cooling period, the most recent of the vast continental ice sheets, known as the Laurentide, began to form across eastern Canada. As it spread and thickened, much of the oceans' waters became trapped in its mass, lowering sea levels by several hundred feet. The visible bulk of Cape Cod is primarily the work of the Wisconsin Stage Glacier, a towering wall of ice 10,000 feet thick that moved south over New England some 25,000 years ago. Grinding forward in rounded fronts, or lobes, the ice sheared off the tops of mountains, gouged huge valleys through granite hills, and plowed up tons upon tons of rocks, material, and debris from what had been the floor of the sea.

Advancing, hesitating, and advancing again, the glacier moved as far south as Long Island, Block Island, Martha's Vineyard, and Nantucket. Then, as the climate warmed, the front edges of the glacier began to melt; the ice sheet retreated north of the present outline of Cape Cod, dropping rocks and large chunks of ice as it went. Then, as cooler

When the glacier melted, it left behind huge rocks, known as erratics, scattered on the landscape.

weather returned, it paused, and, as the flow of ice exceeded the rate of melting, the glacial lobes once more advanced. This time they pushed enormous amounts of drift material across the face of the Upper and Lower Cape, creating the Elizabeth Islands in Buzzards Bay and the rocky, morainal hills on the western and northern sides of the Upper Cape.

As the glacier began its final withdrawal about 18,000 years ago, water from the melting ice carried and sorted finer material, forming the gently sloping southern and interlobate outwash plains of the Upper and Lower Cape (see pages 26-27). Braided meltwater streams covered the ice chunks that the retreating glacier had dropped in thick, insulating layers of outwash material. Eventually, perhaps centuries later, the buried ice melted and the glacial debris above it sank, creating the hundreds of kettle holes that are characteristic of so much of the Cape's topography.

As the great ice sheets melted, the sea level began to rise, forcing the Cape's fresh groundwater upward. When the freshwater level intersected with these kettle holes, the Cape's numerous kettle ponds, so clear and deep, came into being. In some places these meltwater deposits and kettle holes form a highly irregular landscape of hills and hollows, such as the "kame and kettle" fields of Eastham, which can be seen on the bike trail from the Salt Pond Visitor Center to Coast Guard Beach.

Farther north a prominent series of east-west valleys cross the high plains of Wellfleet and Truro, separated by the so-called "hogback" hills of Truro. Most of these valleys only partially cross the Lower Cape. An exception is the Pamet River Valley, which traverses the entire forearm of the Cape, separated from the ocean at its eastern end only by a fragile line of dunes that is sometimes broken through by major storms.

For many years geologists believed these valleys were carved out by glacial meltwater streams, but a more recent theory suggests a different origin, based on a phenomenon known as "spring sapping." Spring sapping occurs when water emerges at the surface of a plain to form a spring, or seep, which then erodes back up the plain toward its head. There is evidence that during the final period of glacial retreat a large freshwater glacial lake existed to the east of Cape Cod. The surface of this lake may have been as much as 80 feet above present sea level, providing a powerful head of water that may have leaked through the porous outwash material of the Lower Cape, producing springs that created the valleys we see today. However they were formed, most of these valley beds are dry today, or else they carry only the small, sluggish streams that constitute Cape Cod's "rivers."

After the glacier's final withdrawal, Cape Cod was only a rough sketch of its present streamlined form. Its moraines, high tablelands, valleys, and kame fields stood high and dry amid the surrounding coastal plain that stretched a hundred miles to the south and east, as far as the present-day Georges Banks.

Kettle ponds formed over time as underground freshwater filled glacial depressions. Today the life in these ponds can be quickly affected by humans.

The sea, however, continued to rise and advance, gradually filling the Gulf of Maine and covering the continental shelf. It probably reached the edge of the glacial Cape some 5,000-6,000 years ago. Now the rough-hewn shapes left by the ice began to undergo a process of planing, smoothing, elaboration, and elongation under the more subtle hands of the sea. Currents, tides, and storms began to chew away at the outer shores of the Lower Cape, creating in time what is surely the most impressive feature of the Seashore, and perhaps the quintessential Cape Cod landscape: the great marine scarp, or sea cliff, of the Outer Beach.

Stretching some 15 miles from Coast Guard Beach in Eastham to Head of the Meadow Beach in North Truro, this curved headland presents a nearly unbroken, undulating bulwark of bold, eroding bluffs, composed of clay and sand and ranging in height from 30 to more than 170 feet above the beach. From South Wellfleet to North Truro the smooth rim of the sea cliff is marked by a half-dozen pronounced dips or "hollows," which are the eroded cross-sections of relict valleys. These hollows were later to play an important part in the human history of this beach.

To the casual observer the cliff face appears uniform, lying at a general "angle of repose" of some 27 degrees to the horizon. But look closely and you will see that, as the Colorado River has done through the Grand Canyon, the sea has cut open the geologic book of the Cape's history, exposing thousands of years of history. Alternating layers of till—rock de-

The Wisconsin Stage Glacier reached into southern New England 25,000 years ago and melted away more than 17,000 years ago, leaving behind moraine and outwash deposits that became the base of Cape Cod, Martha's Vineyard, Nantucket, and the Elizabeth Islands (see illustrations at right). But this was only the latest in a series of Pleistocene glaciers that covered Cape Cod during the past 1.5 million years. Even the deposits of these earlier glaciers may rest on a much older and more

stable land form, a wide, seaward-sloping surface called a coastal plain or, if submerged, a continental shelf. The plain and shelf are underlain by sediments. The shelf was exposed during the ice ages by a concomitant drop in sea level of some 400-500 feet, but today it lies drowned under rising waters. Even more deeply buried, some 500-800 feet beneath the surface, lies the ancient granite bedrock that is so characteristic of most other New England areas. There is evidence that the post-glacial

Outwash Plains and Kettles

As the Buzzards Bay, Cape Cod Bay, and, perhaps, the South Channel glacial lobes waned, they left behind moraines (above right). Melt- *water streams carried sand and gravel that then formed out-* *wash plains beyond the ice (above and below). Sometimes these materials buried*

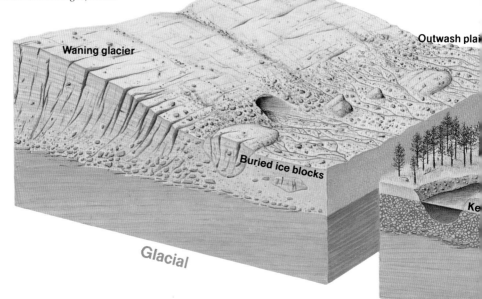

Waning glacier

Outwash plai

Buried ice blocks

Ke

Glacial

Postgla

26

landscape looked very much like arctic tundra. Deep in the bottom of Truro's Great Pond, twigs of arctic willow have been retrieved with 11,000-year-old scale insects still attached to the bark. Caribou, arctic fox, and perhaps musk ox, roamed lichen-covered plains where white-tailed deer and red fox live today. Gradually a boreal forest of spruce and fir took root, much like the forests that now cover northern Canada.

large blocks of ice. In time, the ice blocks melted, leaving steep-sided depressions called kettles that became freshwater ponds if they were deep enough to intersect the water table. Some of these ponds became connected to the sea and turned into salt ponds, such as the one near the Seashore visitor center in Eastham. Over the years peat has filled in many of the ponds.

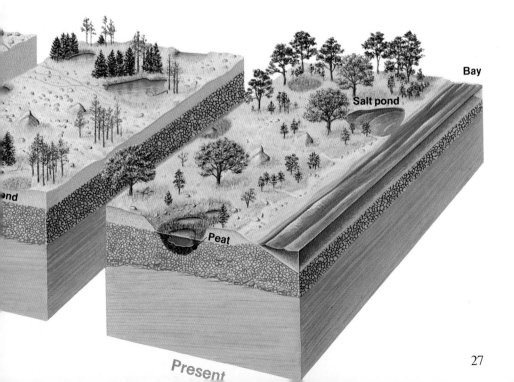

Bay

Salt pond

Peat

nd

Present

27

The Restless Shore

Within a person's lifetime, the Cape's shape changes dramatically. The waters of the ocean and bay and the wind constantly erode material here and deposit it there. Major storms can create islands, sandbars, and dunes and revamp other land forms. A storm in 1931 weakened playwright Eugene O'Neill's home—the old Peaked Hill Bars Coast Guard Station—and sent it into the ocean in 1932 (below). Summer winds generally come from the west or southwest. In the winter, the most severe winds come from the northwest or northeast. The Outer Cape as a whole is moving westward and diminishing as these forces tear at the landscape and as ocean currents move sand northward and southward from about the Marconi Station Site. For every 5 acres of sand eroded, about 2 acres are deposited up or down the coast, thereby elongating (see map at right) the hook at Provincetown and North Beach and Monomoy Point off Chatham. On the bay side, sands have extended Jeremy Point southward to a point almost directly west of Marconi Beach. An 1889 U.S. Coast and Geodetic Survey report says that the entire Outer Beach from 1848 to 1888 lost 323,233,030 cubic yards of earth and sand, enough to cover the 55-acre U.S. Capitol grounds to a depth of 375 feet. Similar changes are taking place today. Some residents have seen North Beach, the southern extension of Nauset Beach, lengthen itself from just south of Orleans to Chatham and then break in 2 pieces in a fierce northeaster in 1987. The

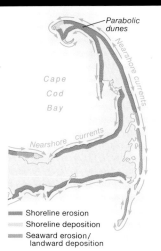

Shoreline erosion
Shoreline deposition
Seaward erosion/
  landward deposition

breach, which has grown to more than a mile in width, has opened Chatham's shoreline to the full force of ocean storms, increasing erosion and claiming more than a dozen houses (inset below). But the breach has also increased tidal flushing of Pleasant Bay, reinvigorating the marine community. In November 1991, a 4-day gale breached the dune line at the head of the Pamet River, carrying sand and saltwater 500 feet into the river.

Parabolic sand dunes occur on the narrow stretch of land east of Pilgrim Lake in the Province Lands of Truro. Prevailing northwest winds blow obliquely to the shoreline and create belts of these unusual dunes with the sands of former beaches.

Low tide bares a wide expanse of sand patterns and tidepools at Coast Guard Beach.

bris deposited by the ice—meltwater-deposited sand and gravel, and clayey silt tell of the glacial advance and withdrawal, of inundation and ebb by the sea. Large outcrops of blue clay, such as the 25-foot thick "Clay Pounds" just north of Highland Light, are the result of glacial lake sediments deposited during the last deglaciation.

The ocean also invaded parts of the land, creating estuaries and embayments at the mouths of these glacial valleys, such as those at Pamet Harbor and Blackfish Creek. Several of the Cape's "salt ponds," such as the one in Eastham below the visitor center, were originally freshwater kettle ponds that have been breached by the rising sea.

As Cape Cod was being smoothed, slimmed, and invaded by the rising sea, it was also being lengthened. Like a sculptor working in clay, the ocean currents took much of the eroded cliff material and, carrying it both north and south, created the elaborate forms of the barrier beaches, barrier islands, and sand hooks that give the Outer Cape its characteristic filigreed coastline. Monomoy Island, North Beach, Nauset Beach, Coast Guard Beach, and Jeremy Point are some of the more prominent of these post-glacial landforms, enclosing such important estuaries as Pleasant Bay, Nauset Harbor, and Wellfleet Harbor. Among the more unusual formations are the tombolos of outer Wellfleet Harbor: the series of short sand beaches that connect Bound Brook, Griffin, Great Beach Hill, and Great Islands.

Of all these sea-spawned parts of Cape Cod, however, the most impressive and extensive is undoubtedly the Provincetown Hook. These 3,000 acres of dunes at the northern tip of the Cape form a broad recurved spit of sand that encloses Provincetown Harbor, one of the finest deepwater harbors on the East Coast and the initial port for the *Mayflower* Pilgrims in 1620. Some oceanographers believe that the hook began to form as much as 6,000 years ago and has built up in a series of roughly parallel ridges, or dune lines, widening out into the ocean.

In the protected bays and inlets behind these elongating fingers of barrier beaches and islands, salt marshes—one of the Cape's most characteristic and important ecosystems—began to form 4,000 to 6,000 years ago. Composed of a few species of salt-tolerant grasses, primarily the stalky cord grass (*Spartina alterniflora*) and the finer salt hay (*Spartina patens*), these green salt meadows of the sea built slowly on the accumulating sediment deposited in protected areas of water by the tides and land runoff. Gradually, as the sea rose relative to the land, the marshes raised and spread themselves on a platform of their own decay, forming thick beds of peat underneath them. As the climate continued to warm, the Cape's woodlands evolved from boreal forests to the mixed pine-oak woodlands we see today.

As the Cape's post-glacial environment grew more diverse and complex, so did the culture of the people living on it. The first Native Americans on Cape Cod are now thought to have arrived at least 9,000 years ago. By the late Archaic Period, starting about 5,000 years ago, local Indian groups had developed a seasonal pattern of movement based on multiple resources. During the warmer months they settled on the shores of bays, marshes, and fish runs, trapping birds and collecting herring and shellfish. In winter they retreated inland to the more protected forested shores of ponds and other wetlands.

By the beginning of the Woodland Period, about 2,500 years ago, Indian settlements had grown even more numerous, larger, and more sedentary. About 800 years ago agriculture and a variety of new materials and tools had been introduced. One of the most important of these "tools" was fire; with it the Cape's Native Americans changed the face of the land.

Many early accounts attest to the extent and scale of the Cape's original woodlands. Even at Provincetown, which must have always been the most barren area of the Outer Cape, the Pilgrim leader William Bradford observed "The whole countrie, full of woods and thickets, wooded with oaks, pines, sassafras, juniper, birch, holly, some ash, walnut, the wood for the most part open and without underwood, fit to go or ride in."

Archeologists now believe that the Cape Cod Indians may have practiced a form of low-level woodland management, burning underbrush, or wooded ridges, to provide browse for game and to make hunting easier. Such burns may have promoted the Cape's characteristic pine barrens, tracts of open woodlands composed primarily of pitch pine, a tree adapted to periodic fires.

Pitch pine is the most common tree on Cape Cod and the only species of native pine that grows in the National Seashore. It survives on well drained glacial sediments and stable sand dunes and is very fire resistant. In this stand on Great Island, the undergrowth is primarily bearberry.

The first human beings to live here did not arrive by sea. In all likelihood they came on foot from the south, southwest, and east, perhaps following caribou or other game up the river valleys across the then wide coastal plain. These people, known as Paleoindians, arrived at least 9,000 years ago. Little is known about them, but they appear to have been a nomadic people, hunting and gathering in small groups. The earliest period represented by a variety of archeological sites is 3,000 to 6,000 BP (Before Present). An archeological site uncovered recent-ly by the ocean at Coast Guard Beach suggests more permanent settlements. This site has been carbon-dated to more than 2,000 BP, and contains post holes indicative of shelter construction. These early Native Americans created chipped stone tools, fished in kettle ponds, and likely wintered in the Cape's coniferous woodlands. By the early 1600s American Indians used or inhabited all the lands now encompassed by Cape Cod National Seashore. These Wampanoags lived in 6 villages along the creeks and bays from Chatham to Wellfleet, re-lying on both the land and sea for food. When French explorer Samuel de Champlain visited Cape Cod in 1605 and 1606, he noted that villagers in what became Eastham and Chatham were raising corn, beans, squash, and tobacco. They tilled their fields with wooden spades after burning off the vegetation. They used crabs as fertilizer but ate clams, quahogs, oysters, and other shellfish. Champlain noted that the Monomoy band at Stage Harbor in Chatham stored corn in grass sacks buried 5 to 6 feet in the sand. He thought they

Native Americans broil fish in this Theodore de Bry 1590 engraving (below) of a John White watercolor. Samuel de Champlain's 1606 map (below right) of Chatham's Stage Harbor area, which he called Port Fortune, shows Wampanoags attacking the French upon learning that they in-tended to settle there. The French had stayed in the harbor for 2 weeks drying out their ship and repairing its rudder.

were better fishermen and farmers than hunters. The Wampanoags lived in domed shelters (below), which consisted of a frame of saplings bent into semicircles. These semicircles were linked by circles of saplings running parallel to the ground. The Indians covered the frames with grass, reeds, and bark and left a large hole in the roofs so smoke could escape from fires in a stone-lined pit in the center. The dwellings were not clustered but separated by cultivated fields.

Henry Botkin's early 20th-century painting depicts the Wampanoags and Pilgrims signing a treaty of friendship.

The *Mayflower* Pilgrims settled in Plymouth—but only after rejecting Cape Cod as unsuitable. On November 9, 1620, these emigrants from England sighted the Cape, the first land they had seen in the 2 months since they left Holland. Though they had intended to continue south and settle in the Hudson River area, they decided, because of treacherous waters off the Cape, to stay. They sailed around the northern end of the Cape, set anchor off what became known as Provincetown, and drew up the "Mayflower Compact," an agreement by which the group of 102, a bare majority of whom were Pilgrims, would govern themselves. During the next month 3 different small groups made "discoveries" of the area. They found a freshwater spring in the Truro area, encountered a few Indians, and discovered several baskets of Indian corn buried on a hill near the Pamet River. On December 6 a group of 19 men led by Myles Standish left the *Mayflower* in a shallop, or small boat, camped for the night in Eastham, and crossed Cape Cod Bay to the mainland. They decided this would be a good place to settle and returned to the ship. On December 16, the *Mayflower* dropped anchor in Plymouth Harbor, and the story of a new English settlement in the New World began. A few passengers and their offspring later settled in the Cape's Eastham area.

Mayflower

Shallop

+
Plymouth Rock

Shallop

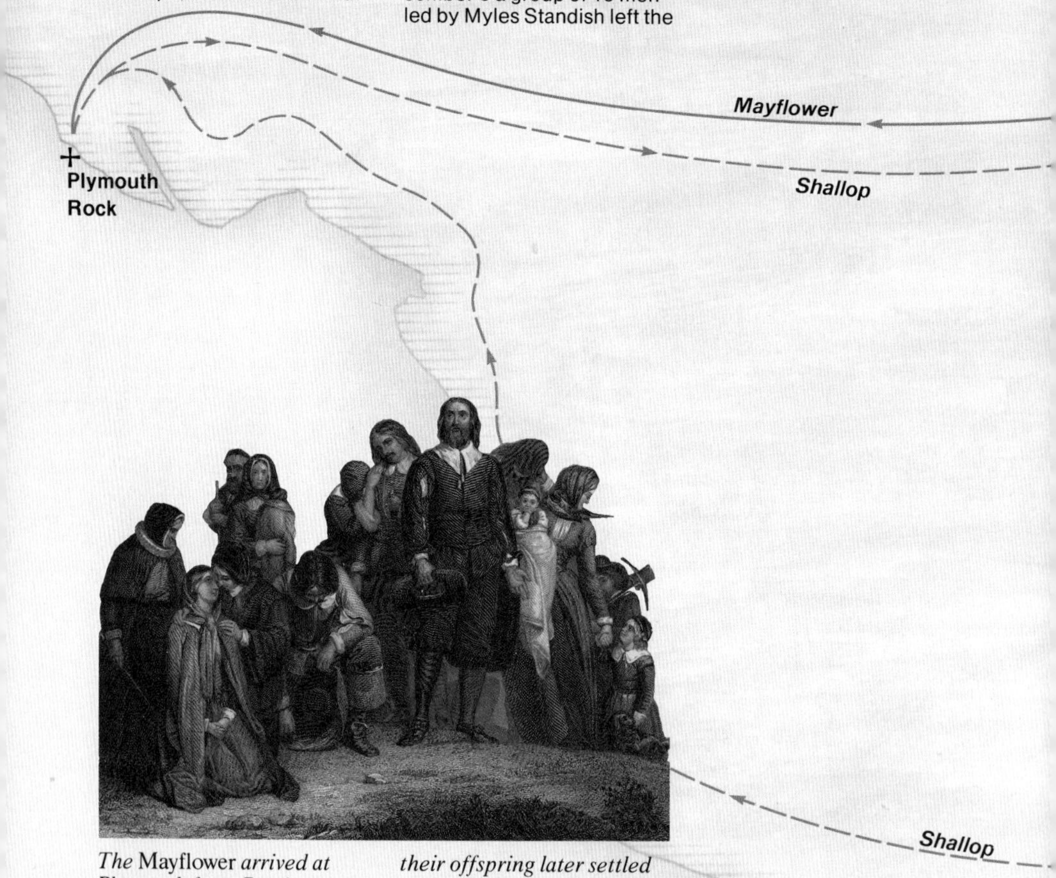

The Mayflower *arrived at Plymouth from Provincetown on December 16, 1620, after failing to cross December 15 because of bad weather. The Pilgrims came ashore on December 18. A few of them and their offspring later settled in the Cape's Eastham area. Graves of* Mayflower *passengers Constance Hopkins Snow, Giles Hopkins, and Joseph Rogers are in Eastham's Old Cove Burying Ground.*

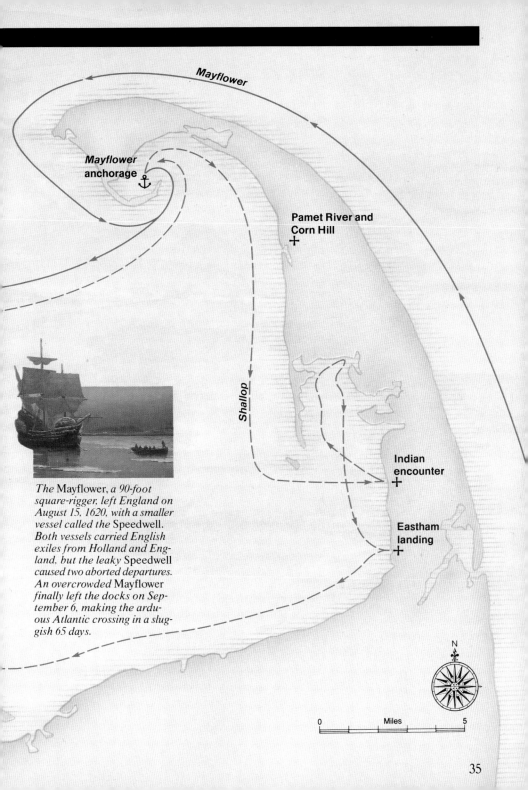

Mayflower

Mayflower anchorage ⚓

Pamet River and Corn Hill ✛

Shallop

Indian encounter ✛

Eastham landing ✛

The Mayflower, *a 90-foot square-rigger, left England on August 15, 1620, with a smaller vessel called the* Speedwell. *Both vessels carried English exiles from Holland and England, but the leaky* Speedwell *caused two aborted departures. An overcrowded* Mayflower *finally left the docks on September 6, making the arduous Atlantic crossing in a sluggish 65 days.*

N

0   Miles   5

In Capt. Myles Standish the Pilgrims had both a military and temporal leader. He helped found the Plymouth Colony, led a group that bought the colony from London investors, and served as assistant governor and treasurer for 5 years. Metacomet, or King Philip, shown in an engraving by Paul Revere, was killed leading the Wampanoags in an unsuccessful war concerning land disputes with the English settlers in 1676.

Some glacial lands, now vanished, still existed in historical times. There are many early references, for example, to Ile Nauset, or Nauset Isle, a point of land that lay off Nauset Beach, perpendicular to the coastline. It may have formed part of Cape Mallebarre, the place of "dangerous shoals and roaring breakers" that turned back the *Mayflower* from its intended destination of Virginia. Nauset Isle had sunk beneath the waves by the 18th century, but another piece of early glacial real estate survived much longer. In the late 19th century, Billingsgate Island, off Jeremy Point in Wellfleet, was a flourishing 60-acre fishing community with livestock, a schoolhouse, and a lighthouse. By 1915, however, the island had been abandoned, and by 1942 it had vanished, the victim of gradual erosion by currents, storms, and rising sea levels. Today, at low tide, one can view the remains of this Wellfleetian Atlantis from the southern bluffs of Great Beach Hill: an extensive spread of granite boulders brought over on ships as riprap in a futile attempt to stem the tides.

To get some idea of the scope of erosion on the Outer Beach, consider this: in 1990 an ancient prehistoric site was uncovered at Coast Guard Beach; archeologists have estimated that at the time of its occupation, nearly 9,000 years ago, it was five miles inland. More recent evidence of erosion can often be observed on the Seashore's ocean side. At Nauset Light Beach, a circular brick foundation from one of the former "Three Sisters" lighthouses (replaced in 1923 with the present single light) is frequently uncovered in winter at the base of the cliffs, having survived a 50-foot slide to the beach. Farther north, at the Marconi Site in South Wellfleet, Guglielmo Marconi constructed his original transmitting towers in 1901-1902, set back 165 feet from the edge of the cliff. Today only two of the foundations remain; the other two have fallen into the sea.

Few things remain in place on the edge of the cliffs or on the dunes. They either move or disappear. Cape Cod Light, first built in 1796, has been replaced twice; the current tower sits some 600 feet back from the site of the original one, though only a little more than 100 feet from the present cliff edge. The present Eastham Coast Guard Station, built in 1936, is a successor to the first one, which succumbed to beach erosion. When the Seashore was established in 1961, more than 80 cottages existed on its barrier beaches. Today, as a result of subsequent storms, less than one quarter of them remain.

Logs and other objects, including the remains of old shipwrecks, are frequently uncovered by eroding dunes and beaches. During a dramatic storm, while he was staying in the Outermost House in the 1920s, Henry Beston described how the blackened skeleton of an ancient ship that had been buried in a dune for more than a century "floated and lifted itself free . . . thus stirring from its grave and yielding its bones again to the fury of the gale."

One survivor of this coastal erosion is the Old Harbor Life Saving Station. Now a maritime museum at Race Point Beach in Provincetown, it began life in 1897 twenty miles to the south on Chatham's North Beach. In 1977, in the face of imminent destruction, the station was cut in half and floated on two barges to its present site.

During the summer, the beaches of the Outer Cape present a generally peaceful and benign aspect. A wide, gently sloping shelf of sand lies between the base of the sea cliffs and a rhythmic, moderate surf. The summer shoreline's peaceful countenance encourages the illusion that all this change and rearrangement of shoreline lies in the settled past. There is little indication to the summer visitor of the ferocity, violence, and transformation that visit this coast in the "off season." But if one returns in late autumn, when the prevailing winds shift to the north and the east, when the first northeasters of the season begin to chew away at the wide summer beach, replacing it with a short, steep winter berm, one begins to have a sense that this is still a land in the making, that, as Henry Beston observed, "Creation is here and now."

In winter the ocean storms claw into the base of these cliffs, undermining them. Along some stretches erosion is gradual, with little rivulets of sand running down the cliff face into the sea. At other places, especially where there are large deposits of clay, the process can be dramatic. Whole slabs of the marine scarp may shelve off at once, and a single stretch of cliff may lose 30 or 40 feet in one storm. In still other areas the beach appears to be accreting, with wide terraces of sand covered with beach grass building out from the cliff base. But overall the Outer Beach

Fall and winter storms often develop quickly and tear away at the shorelines, removing sands from one place and depositing them elsewhere.

The Cape Cod House

If anything distinguishes Cape Cod nationally, it's a house style. Essentially the Cape Cod House is a modest story-and-a-half frame structure that hugs the ground and has a steep roof that sheds the rain and snow and provides protection from buffeting winds. Usually the wooden shingles on the sides are left unpainted, and thus the sides—and the roof—take on a natural grayish to dark brown patina depending on the effects of the sun and wind-driven sands and salt.

Sometimes the front, shingle or clapboard, may be painted, and if so most likely white. Many of the oldest Capes were built in stages. A half house might become a three-quarter and later on a full house, depending on the needs or wealth of the family. A full Cape, such as the park's Atwood-Higgins House (right and cutaway below), is deceiving: it has much more room than you might expect from its external appearance. Inside the front door is a small hallway or entryway. To

the left and the right are small parlors. In the center of the back is a large keeping room, or kitchen, that later was divided into 2 rooms, where most of the daily household activity took place. At both ends of the kitchen are a buttery, or pantry, and a bedroom, or a borning room. At the center of the house is an intricately-designed brick chimney serving fireplaces in the parlors, kitchen, and front hall.

The chimney divides the upstairs into 2 bedrooms, probably for children. The eastern part (right) of the Atwood-Higgins House was built in Wellfleet about 1730 by Thomas Higgins; the western side was built about the same time but attached later. The house remained in the Higgins family until 1805, when Thomas Atwood became the owner. The Higgins family later regained ownership.

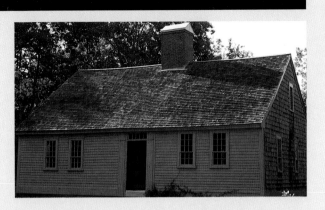

The half house version of the Cape Cod House has 2 windows to the left or right of the front door. The three-quarter house has a third on the other side of the door, and the full Cape has 2 on each side.

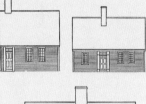

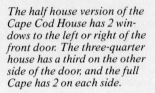

The post-and-beam construction method used in the Atwood-Higgins House was commonly used on Cape Cod until the early 1800s. Posts and beams were put together by mortising a hole in one and inserting a tenon from the other.

39

continues to erode, losing an average of three feet a year.

On the barrier beaches the erosion process is somewhat different, though the overall effect is also retreat. Barrier beach dune lines are dynamic systems. That is, they retreat and maintain themselves by moving with, rather than resisting, the ocean's power. Normally the foreslopes of the dunes flatten out during a severe storm, presenting a less steep face to the waves, which helps to dissipate their force. Meanwhile wind and occasional storm surges that break through the line carry sand into the estuary or marsh behind the dunes. These deposits are gradually colonized by beach grass and other beach plants, which begin the process of building up another dune line as the foredunes continue to erode. Evidence of this gradual retreat can be observed by the occasional emergence in front of the present dune lines of peat ledges, the remains of a salt marsh or freshwater bog that once lay behind a former line of dunes. In a healthy system and under normal conditions a barrier beach "rolls over on itself" in a smooth progression landward.

On occasion, however, even this process is overwhelmed by an unusual manifestation of the sea's power. One such manifestation was the Great Blizzard of February 6-7, 1978, called "The Storm of the Century." Carrying 15-foot tides and hurricane-force winds, this storm rearranged many parts of the Cape's shoreline. Monomoy Island, for example, was severed in two, and remains so today. But nowhere were the effects more dramatic and visible than at Eastham's Coast Guard Beach. Storm surges breached the dune line, flattening 90 percent of the dunes themselves, carrying off most of the beach cottages, including Henry Beston's Outermost House, and totally destroying the Seashore's bathhouse and large parking lot.

Provincetown has always been the Cape community that has had to contend most with change. During the 19th century the moving dunes of the Province Lands threatened to bury its houses and silt up its vital harbor. Subsequent erosion control and beach grass plantings have so far kept the dunes at bay, but a more implacable force may now be threatening the town.

Over the past few decades oceanographers have

observed an acceleration in the rate of sea level rise, possibly the result of global warming. The sea may now be rising as much as one foot every century, which on low shorelines translates into a loss of 100 feet inland. Nowhere on Cape Cod does thick settlement lie so close to the shore as along the low, narrow streets of Provincetown. If present rises in the level of the sea continue, or, as seems likely, increase, the ocean may well claim this ancient fishing community before the dunes do.

Meanwhile the bulk of the Provincetown Hook continues to expand outward into the sea. The dangerous Peaked Hill Bars represent, in current oceanographic theory, the next ridge of Province Lands dunes in the making, rising gradually from the sea. But regardless of such gains, or the pains taken by humans to stem the loss of land from the sea, the Cape is inevitably losing more than it is replacing. Oceanographers estimate that for every five acres of shoreline lost to erosion, only two are replaced with new land in the form of barrier beaches or sand hooks. There is little doubt that the Cape's ultimate fate is to return to the sea that spawned and shaped it. At current rates of sea-level rise, Cape Cod has at best only another five to six thousand years before the Puritan preacher Cotton Mather's prediction comes true, and "shoals of codfish be seen swimming on its highest hills."

Salt Marsh

Salt hay and cord grass

Moon snail

Sea stars

Fiddler crab

Lobster

Anemone

Hermit crab

Moon jelly

42

Sea-lavender and honey bee

Northern diamondback terrapin

Bay scallop

Glasswort, or salicornia

Eelgrass

Sea robin

Rock crabs

Sea lettuce and mussels

The Bountiful Sea

Schools of silversides, about 3 inches long, dart through shallow waters feeding on plankton. They in turn are fed upon by other marine life and birds such as gulls and terns.

The first English settlers who came to the Cape from Plymouth in 1639 were farmers, not fishermen. It took several generations for them to give themselves fully to the life of the sea, though they early saw the potential in it. In fact, even in their farming they quickly took advantage of what the sea had to offer. Alewives were gathered from local streams in spring as a seasonal source of food, as well as fertilizer for their cornfields, a practice taught to them by the Wampanoag Indians. Eelgrass from the flats also provided fertilizer, mulch, insulation for house foundations, and even stuffing for mattresses. Lobsters were so abundant that they were often blown ashore in deep windrows. They were more valued as fertilizer than food in colonial times, and in the 18th century a petition was filed with the General Court on behalf of indentured servants that they "not be fed lobsters more than twice a week"!

Even more valued by these early Cape Cod farmers were the salt marshes, or salt meadows. In a place of little natural grassland, marshes were prized for grazing. During the spring and summer cows were pastured on the marshes, with boys sent along to keep them from falling into the tidal creeks or potholes, called "pannes." In fall the salt hay was scythed, stacked in ricks on raised wooden platforms called "staddles," and hauled to the barns by oxen or horses wearing special wide wooden shoes to keep them from sinking into the peat.

The Cape's numerous bays, inlets, salt ponds, and estuaries were also early recognized as marine cornucopias. Foot-long oysters, scallops, crabs, eels, flounder, diamondback terrapins, striped bass, mackerel, and other fish were taken for local use, and clam shells provided the lime for plastering colonial walls.

Still, despite the many uses these early settlers made of the marine riches around them, they did not truly become men of the sea until they were forced

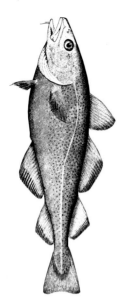

The Atlantic cod typically weighs 10 to 25 pounds but ranges up to 200 pounds. Its bountiful numbers sparked Massachusetts' first major maritime industry in the 1600s. A bottom dweller, the cod soon attracted Cape fishermen to the Grand Banks off Newfoundland and to Georges Bank off Cape Cod.

to by the land's limitations and by their own mismanagement of it. The Cape's once-abundant woodlands were cut and burned for farm and pasture land and consumed for a seemingly endless array of local uses and industries: heating homes; boiling seawater for salt; building boats, gristmills, houses, and barns; firing tar kilns; and trying out whale blubber, to name just a few.

The thin glacial soil, exhausted by repeated cropping and left unprotected by deforestation, soon blew away. In Provincetown, unregulated cutting and grazing in the Province Lands let loose the dunes, which threatened to bury the town and fill up the harbor. By 1800 dune ridges were advancing at a rate of 90 feet a year. In 1847 Massachusetts geologist Edward Hitchcock, visiting the Lower Cape, felt as if he were "in the depths of an Arabian or Libyan desert."

Though the Cape's soil was never very rich, the waters around it teemed with abundance, and in the sea Cape Codders found their true destiny. Thrust some 30 miles out into the Atlantic, the Cape partakes of two distinct marine environments. Cape Cod Bay is part of the larger Gulf of Maine ecosystem, a cold-water habitat influenced by the south-flowing Labrador Current. The waters of Nantucket Sound, averaging some ten degrees warmer, are influenced primarily by the northward-flowing Gulf Stream.

Such a range of temperature in its surrounding waters, combined with numerous estuaries of varying salinity, has produced one of the richest diversities of marine habitats on the East Coast. A National Park Service report states that the difference in flora and fauna "between Cape Cod Bay and Buzzards Bay is greater than that between Cape Cod Bay and the Bay of Fundy, or between Buzzards Bay and the coast of Virginia." Warm-water species such as whelks, bay scallops, diamondback terrapins, blue crabs, striped bass and tuna inhabit the same waters as do more northerly species such as blue mussels, Jonah crabs, winter flounder, halibut, and, of course, cod.

Of all the creatures nourished by the sea, none has been more important to the history of Cape Cod than the Atlantic cod, *Gadus morhua*. In 1602, the English explorer Bartholomew Gosnold was so impressed by the schools of codfish surrounding his vessel, the *Concord*, that he named this peninsula after them, a name so apt that, in the words of Truro historian Shebnah Rich, "blow high or low, cold or hot, thick or thin, fish or no fish, it has hung on like a lamper-eel from that day to this."

The cod has always been what Captain John Smith described in 1616 as "the maine staple" of the New England fishing industry. More than a century before the *Mayflower* landed, fleets of small ships from Holland, Portugal, and the Basque region of Spain had braved the North Atlantic annually to fish the rich spawning grounds of the Grand Banks of Newfoundland, salting their fish ashore and returning with their catch to European ports. It is more than likely that the first European visitors to Provincetown Harbor—originally called Cape Cod Harbor—were Portuguese fishermen who came ashore to cure, or "make," cod on the long sandy stretches there. Some permanent European settlements may even have existed there in the 1500s.

If the Plymouth settlers were unskilled as fishermen, they were smart enough to sell the rights to fish to others, and in 1670 a tax on the Provincetown fisheries was established as a means of funding public schools in Plymouth. As Thoreau put it, schools of fish were used to provide schools for children. As early as 1730, however, Cape fishing captains were making voyages to the Grand Banks in a "triangle trade:" taking salted cod to the West Indies, exchanging fish for molasses and rum, and bringing them back to the mainland where they were sold to finance new and larger ships for more fishing trips. But during the 18th century most fishing remained inshore, or close to shore, and part-time. Cape Codders remained half-farmers, half-fishermen, and most took only enough for themselves and local markets.

The British embargo on shipping during the American Revolution was disastrous for the Cape's nascent fishing industry, but after the war it began to come into its own. Shorter and more profitable runs were made in smaller boats, and lightly salted "fresh" fish was brought directly back for sale in Boston. Fish flakes—low wooden slatted platforms on which split cod was salted and sun-dried—became the common method of curing fish. Because of its capacious harbor, "where a thousand sail may safely

A few Pilgrims left Plymouth and returned to the Cape and settled in the Eastham area. So, too, did this windmill. It was built in Plymouth in the 1600s and was moved to Eastham in 1793. The mill was used in producing flour. Some mills were used to pump seawater as a part of saltworks.

Wellfleet and Provincetown were Cape Cod's premier whaling ports in the late 1700s and early 1800s. Some whaling ships sailed out of other Cape towns, but these 2 ports were crowded and bustling with ships and crews and related tradesmen and merchants. Both places eventually gave way to Nantucket and New Bedford, but many Cape captains continued to pursue the leviathan in distant seas. Settlers had been intrigued by whales since Native Americans taught them how to use beached whales for food and oil not long after the *Mayflower* anchored in Cape Cod Bay. They soon erected towers on beaches to look out for whales, which they would pursue in small boats along the coasts. As whale oil grew in importance as a lighting fluid and as whale bone and baleen were used for more household and personal products, sloops and small schooners gave way to larger schooners and square-riggers, such as barks, and even full-rigged ships. And the ships extended their hunting grounds first to the South Atlantic and then to the Pacific and Arctic oceans as their

In this painting, a sperm whale overturns a whaleboat crew that has harpooned it.

Harpoon styles improved over the years. Early harpoons were double-flued (left). Later refinements included the toggle head, invented in 1848, which was less likely to come loose from the whale.

quarry changed from right whales to sperm whales and bowheads. Whaling's peak years were between 1825 and 1860. The decline is traced to the discovery of petroleum in Pennsylvania in 1859, the loss of many ships in the Civil War, and a surge in other fisheries. Edward Penniman of Eastham went to sea at age 11 in 1842 as a cook and at age 21 as a harpooner aboard the New Bedford whaleship *Isabella*. By 1860 he was captain of the bark *Minerva*. When he retired in 1883, he had made 6 voyages as a whaling captain.

While whaling crews were on long sea voyages, many of the men whiled away the time making scrimshaw objects, including such intricate pieces as this sewing box.

When Augusta Penniman accompanied her husband on voyages, she kept detailed whaling-trip logs in which she used symbols to indicate kills and misses. In 1868 the Pennimans built a French Second Empire mansard-roofed house (above) with a cupola overlooking the ocean and bay in Eastham. The Penniman House, now a part of the National Seashore, sports a pair of whale jaws at the entrance to its walk.

49

Coastal packet boats, the first commercial vessels on Cape Cod, flourished in the first half of the 19th century carrying mail, passengers, salt, and other cargo to Boston and New York. These boats were built in local yards from local lumber and captained by local men. The rivalry and pride among the various Cape towns for the fastest and most seaworthy packets stood the Cape men in good stead when the new Republic began to engage in international trade. Cape Codders, in fact, were among the first to sail the American flag into many foreign ports and uncharted seas. Captain John Kendrick of Harwich sailed from Boston in 1787 in the *Columbia*, the first American ship to circumnavigate the globe. A Brewster captain, Elijah Cobb, was captured by a French frigate during the French Revolution and made a successful appeal to Robespierre for release. After the War of 1812, many Cape Codders captained the first of the trans-Atlantic Liverpool packets. But their true glory awaited them on the decks of the clipper ships, those majestic sailing vessels of the 1840s and '50s. With their sleek hulls and tapered sterns, towering masts and double courses of sails, their speed and maneuverability in sailing into the wind, the "Yankee clippers" were generally regarded as the finest wooden ships ever made. They counted scores of Cape

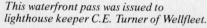

COLEMAN'S
California Line FOR San Francisco

To sail positively on or before the advertised day.

Ship of the 21st of February.

THE ELEGANT & FAVORITE CLIPPER SHIP

OSBORN HOWES

KELLEY, Commander.

Having been for several days at her berth, Pier 9, East River, receiving cargo, we are now prepared to despatch her positively as above. Her superiority over all other clippers now loading, is acknowledged, and the insures at the lowest rates.
Shippers will please hand in their Bills of Lading for signature as soon as shipments are completed For Freight, apply to
WM. T. COLEMAN & CO.,
88 WALL STREET, Tontine Building
N B.—Ships of this line take no freight after the advertised day.
Agents at San Francisco, Messrs. WM. T. COLEMAN & CO.

Nesbitt & Co., Printers.

This waterfront pass was issued to lighthouse keeper C.E. Turner of Wellfleet.

WATER-FRONT PASS.

Port of *Massachusett*
Pass *C E Turner*
Residence *Wellfleet Mass*
Nationality *American*
Occupation *Keeper*
Employed by
Location *Universal*

Date

No. **480281**

United States Mar

This sailing card is for a clipper ship named after its owner, Osborn Howes, a Dennis native who with his brother-in-law ran an international shipping fleet out of Boston in the 1800s. He managed or owned 43 vessels in his 87 years.

Codders among their captains, many of whom set transoceanic sailing records that still stand today. To cite only one, and not the most modest example, the following gravestone for Freeman Hatch, 1820-89, can be found in an Eastham cemetery: "He became famous making the astonishing passage in the clipper ship *Northern Light* from San Francisco in 76 days 6 hours—an achievement won by no mortal before or since."

Asa Eldridge (right) of Yarmouth served as captain of the clipper ship Red Jacket *(above) when it set a record crossing from New York to Liverpool of 13 days, 1 hour. Eldridge was lost in the North Atlantic in February 1856 with the steamer* Pacific.

Decked out in top hats about 1855, Brewster sea captains Charles Crosby (left) and James Edwin Crosby flank an unidentified English captain.

Sailors in the 19th century used octants to determine their latitude by measuring the sun's angle above the horizon at noon. Tables converted that figure for the day, month, and year into distance north or south of the equator.

51

The whaler Charles W. Morgan *can be toured today at Mystic Seaport in Connecticut.*

anchor," and its extensive sandy beaches providing ideal sites for fish flakes, Provincetown soon became a magnet for the Cape's burgeoning fish exports. From a mere ten houses in 1755, it boasted a thousand residents in 1802, and by 1840 the Cape-tip community had become the preeminent fishing port on Cape Cod, harboring more than 100 cod trawlers. When Thoreau visited its narrow streets in 1849, he counted over 200 mackerel schooners alone.

One of the major events in the growth of the Cape's fishing industry was the opening up of the Georges Banks in 1821. Much closer than Newfoundland's Grand Banks, but just as fertile, this vast glacial deposit, the work of the same ice sheets that formed Cape Cod, had long been shunned because of its dangerous shoals and currents. But the rising price of cod and halibut tempted more and more fishing captains to its waters. By the mid-1800s a distinctive "banker" version of the Provincetown schooner had evolved, sleeker and faster than the old tub-hulled vessels, giving greater maneuverability on the shoals and greater speed in getting the fish to market first for the best prices. The schooners also began carrying dories aboard. These small, double-ended, highly seaworthy boats were launched from the mother ship with two-man crews, who set out hundreds of yards of hooked lines on floats, hauled in their catch by hand, and waited to be picked up at the end of the day. Deep-sea dory fishing, though it greatly increased the yield of each voyage, also increased the risks for the crews, especially if, as frequently happened, these small rowboats became separated from the schooners in fog or squalls.

After the Civil War the industrial revolution hit the fishing market. Greater concentrations of capital, larger boats, more expensive gear and faster transportation for landed fish were required. Most Cape towns did not possess the resources, the anchorage, or the facilities to compete. They turned instead to local handlining, trap, and weir fishing, or, as in Wellfleet's case, began to develop local shellfish industries. But Provincetown, reinvigorated by the arrival of the railroad in 1873 and by an influx of Portuguese fishermen from the Azores in the late 1800s, remained a prominent New England fishing port until the end of the century, when the increasing demands of capital investment and labor forced the town to yield to the ports of Boston and Gloucester.

Today Provincetown, Chatham, and several of the other Cape towns still support small but tenacious fleets of local draggers, trawlers, and lobster boats. Declining stocks, smaller quotas, oil spills, competition from foreign "factory ships," and ever-more-expensive gear have made it even harder for the small fisherman to stay in business. But the independence, challenge, the hope of a "big haul," and the unexplainable lure of the sea continue to attract local residents to this ancient profession, and it is likely they will continue to do so as long as there are fish to catch.

Though whaling was never as important to Cape Cod as were its fisheries, it nonetheless formed an significant chapter in the Cape's maritime history. In the early colonial days drift whales came ashore frequently enough that they formed a portion of some Congregational ministers' salaries. Live whales were common in Cape Cod Bay and Nantucket Sound, and a modest inshore whaling industry developed in the 17th century. In fact, in 1694 a Yarmouth captain, Ichabod Paddock, was invited to Nantucket to teach the Quaker residents the trade. He apparently did such a good job that Nantucketers soon became the preeminent New England whalers.

Try yards—areas where whale blubber was boiled down, or "tried out," to obtain the oil—were established early in the 18th century on Barnstable's Sandy Neck, and in 1715 that town boasted some 200 inshore whalers. But such intensive exploitation soon diminished the nearby stocks, and by 1750 the inshore whaling industry was dying out.

As in fishing, so in whaling, Provincetown with its unrivaled harbor became the Cape's most important port. At its peak, in 1876, seventeen deep-sea whaling vessels sailed out of Provincetown. The last two Cape whaling vessels made their final voyages from Provincetown in 1920-21. They were the schooner *Cameo* and the bark *Charles W. Morgan*. The *Morgan* is preserved at Mystic Seaport in Connecticut.

One species of cetacean has had a peculiar attachment to the Cape shores over the centuries. The pilot whale, or blackfish, is a medium-sized toothed whale, 15-22 feet in length. It tends to travel in tight groups, and large numbers of pilot whales frequently strand themselves in the tidal creeks and on the

Colorful boats line up in Provincetown harbor ready for another day of commercial fishing.

As the name implies, Cape Cod and fishing are nearly synonymous. The Wampanoag Indians were primarily farmers, but they also dug clams, gathered oysters and scallops, caught crabs, and fished for herring and others fishes, mostly in freshwater or where it mixed with saltwater. They used bone hooks, spears, nets made of plant fibers, and wooden-staked weirs. The first European settlers on the Cape also were farmers, but they soon learned how bountiful the sea was and quickly refined and developed various kinds of fisheries. "I confess I was surprised to find that so many men spent their whole day, ay, their whole lives almost, a-fishing," Henry David Thoreau observed in the mid-1800s. How they fished, where they fished, and what they fished for have changed greatly over the years as some species were over-fished and as technological changes were introduced. The Atlantic cod was the first fish to spark a major industry. In 1878, 63 vessels sailed out of Provincetown in search of cod and returned with more than 7.5 million pounds. Wellfleet led the Cape in fishing for mackerel; in 1879, 30 schooners followed the schools north May to November from North Carolina to Maine. The ships returned to Cape ports from long voyages with their catches salted and dried for market. After brief trips, the fish were dried on the docks in Provincetown and other ports (below left and continuing counterclockwise). Hard-shelled clams—called quahogs and pronounced as ko-hogs by Cape Codders—were and are harvested in deep water with wooden-handled rakes up to 56 feet in length. Sometimes nets were stretched between poles to form weirs; high tides would bring the fish in; and at

low tide men would go out— sometimes with wagons and horses—to remove their catches. Early on fishermen used small boats or dories to fish with lines, then with nets and wooden traps, in nearby waters; trawling schooners carried dories to the fishing grounds of the banks for cod, haddock, and groundfish. At first lobsters were so plentiful they were used as bait and then as food for servants; today they are not plentiful and are among the highest-priced seafood in America. Fishermen in small boats still go out to pull up lobster traps.

Saltworks

The growth in Cape Cod's fishing industry early in the 19th century spawned other sea-related industries. One of the most important was the development of the saltworks. Salt was needed especially to preserve the cod and mackerel and other fish caught at such distant places as the Grand Banks. In colonial times, salt was obtained by boiling seawater in enormous iron pots that were set up near the beach, a technique that hastened the demise of the Cape's forests.

But as early as 1776, Captain John Sears of Dennis had experimented with making salt through evaporation of seawater in long shallow troughs. With a bushel of salt worth a dollar at the turn of the century, saltmaking became profitable and Cape Codders continued to improve their methods. They incorporated movable roofs on rails (right) to cover the troughs on cloudy or rainy days, windmills to pump seawater through hollow wooden pipes into the troughs, and an intricate system of reservoirs,

falls, vats, and boiling rooms. The water went through three stages: evaporation, precipitation of lime, and crystallization of salt. Epsom salts came from boiling "bitter water," the liquid remaining after the salt was crystallized. During the 1830s saltworks were a major industry in almost every Cape town, covering dozens of acres of beaches (background engraving). At their peak on Cape Cod, there were 442 saltworks producing more than 500,000 bushels of salt a year. By 1840, however, the opening up of large salt mines in the West, among other factors, signaled the beginning of the industry's swift decline. Still, in the 1850s, Henry David Thoreau saw "saltworks scattered all along the shore, with their long rows of vats resting on piles driven into the marsh, their low, turtle-like roofs, and their . . . wind-mills . . . novel and interesting objects to an inlander."

A humpback whale displays its tail stock and flukes off the Provincetown coast. Other species of whales are also commonly seen from spring through fall, including finback, minke, and right whales. These marine mammals, once hunted for their blubber and baleen, now support a thriving whale-watching industry.

shallow flats of Cape Cod Bay, particularly in the labyrinthine channels around Wellfleet Harbor. Scientists are still trying to fathom the causes of these mass strandings, but to the early Cape Codders they were obviously a gift from God, providing both meat and high-grade whale oil from the rounded "melon" in the front of the whale's head.

Before long lookouts were posted to spot pods of pilot whales coming inshore. Fleets of small boats would then be launched, and their crew members would circle the whales and beat their oars and blow horns to "help" the panicked herd ashore. In 1855 Thoreau witnessed hundreds of blackfish driven ashore at Great Hollow in Truro, and in 1880 a school of more than 1,300 stranded in South Wellfleet at Blackfish Creek, giving it its present name. Strandings of pilot whales continued to be a source of local income for Cape towns into the 1930s, when, for reasons not clear, they largely disappeared. But since the mid-1970s strandings have become common again; in November 1982, sixty-five pilot whales came ashore at Wellfleet's Lieutenant Island.

In the eyes of many, Cape Codders attained their greatest seafaring eminence as shipmasters in the merchant marine. As captains during the early days of the Republic, they were, as Cape historian Henry Kittredge noted, "the first ambassadors of a young nation." Later, in command of the great clipper ships of the mid-19th-century, they set a number of transoceanic sailing records that still stand today. They also made considerable fortunes for their owners, and for themselves. This monetary bounty was translated into the hundreds of substantial "captain's houses" that still stand along the streets of their home towns from Sandwich to Provincetown. Brewster alone is said to have counted more than 50 sea captains residing there at one time.

But perhaps even more important than the fortunes and exotic souvenirs these ship captains brought home from foreign ports was the broad perspective gained by their experience. It was said that many a Cape Codder had been to China who had never gone to Boston by land. Wives and children often sailed with the shipmasters, and several of Cape Cod's small villages boasted a cosmopolitan culture unusual among mid-19th-century New England towns. Many of the retired ship captains became selectmen in their towns, and, as Kittredge put it, "Narrow-mindedness found barren soil in a district where two houses out of every three belonged to men who knew half the seaports of the world and had lived ashore for months at a time in foreign countries."

But the sea that brought such bounty and prosperity to Cape Codders during the years between the War of 1812 and the Civil War was not always kind. There was a dark side to the Cape's relationship to the ocean, a side reflected in the numerous slate and limestone markers in the Cape's small burying grounds that bear the inscription "Lost at Sea."

The 30-mile stretch of land between the Monomoy Shoals on the south and Race Point on the north is one of several East Coast stretches known as "Graveyards of the Atlantic." The Cape's sandy outer shore does not look as menacing as, say, the rocky coastline of Maine or Nova Scotia. Its threats take more subtle shapes, in the form of submerged sandbars and treacherous rips, that can easily run a ship aground, and where in winter gales waves will pound a vessel to pieces as effectively as if it were on solid rock.

The first recorded shipwreck on Cape Cod was the *Sparrowhawk*, an English vessel that struck a sandbar off Orleans in 1626. Since then an estimated 3,000 vessels have been lost in the waters off the Cape, most on the stretch of open Atlantic from Chatham to Provincetown. One of the most famous of the early wrecks was the pirate ship *Whydah*, a 300-ton galley commanded by "Black Sam" Bellamy, which broke up on the bars off Eastham (now South Wellfleet) on May 8, 1717. More than 145 lives were lost in the wreck, and of the nine survivors, seven were tried for piracy and hanged on Boston Common.

Cape Codders early on recognized that those who went "down to the sea in ships" did not always come back. The most deadly areas were the shoals and rips off Monomoy—places known as "Cape Mallebarre" and "Tucker's Terror"—and the infamous Peaked Hill Bars off the Atlantic, or back side, of Provincetown. Not all losses occurred close to shore, however. Once fishing vessels began making trips to the Georges and Grand Banks, entire fleets were sometimes caught in furious fall northeasters, winter gales, and hurricanes. Perhaps the worst single storm, in terms of its effects on local Cape communities, was the disastrous October Gale of 1841. Dozens of

Over the years the sea has taken the life of many a Cape Cod fisherman. This stone, in the Burying Ground of the First Congregational Parish of Truro, honors Mrs. Rebecca Snow, who died Nov. 4, 1832, and her husband, Capt. Reuben Snow, who was lost at sea in January 1825. The inscription at the bottom reads: "Tho' in the dust, or in the sea, their mortal bodies rest, their spirits dwell in paradise."

About 3,000 ships and small fishing boats have wrecked in heavy fog or storms along the Cape's coastline. Periodic northeasters and occasional hurricanes pound the coast and drive ships upon sandbars—more than 1,000 of them between 1843 and 1903 alone. One of the first recorded wrecks occurred December 17, 1626, when the Virginia-bound *Sparrowhawk* ran aground off Orleans. A gale then forced the ship over the sandbar and grounded it in the harbor. The ship was repaired, but another

This map shows the locations of Cape shipwrecks between 1802 and 1967. The schooner Messenger *(top) of Boston lost its masts in a storm off Long Island in 1894; weeks later the hull washed ashore in Wellfleet. Sailing out of Salem, the* Ulysses *(right) was grounded with 2 other ships off the Cape on February 22, 1803. After struggling ashore, 87 men froze to death.*

storm caused so much damage it was abandoned. In 1863 a storm removed sand from the wreck, and the remains were taken later to the Pilgrim Hall Museum in Plymouth. The *Sparrowhawk's* passengers survived their ordeal, but many have not been so fortunate. More than 145 lives were lost when the pirate ship *Whydah* sank off Wellfleet in 1717. The most lost in any wreck were all 175 passengers and crew who went down off Truro with the steamship *Portland* in a huge gale November 27, 1898. Such storms have turned many fishermen's wives into widows. Of the women living in Barnstable County in 1839, nearly 1,000 had lost husbands at sea. In one of the worst disasters, only 2 of Truro's 9 fishing fleet crews survived a gale on October 3, 1841; 57 fishermen were drowned, and 9 of them were 11 to 14 years old. The storm left 19 Truro widows with 39 children. Dennis lost 20 men and Yarmouth lost 10. Some military ships and large liners also have gone down in Cape waters. On December 17, 1927, the Coast Guard cutter *Paulding* collided with a Navy submarine as it surfaced off Wood End at Provincetown's tip. Divers found that 6 of the 40 submariners initially survived, but they perished as a gale hampered rescue efforts.

In 1956 the Italian passenger liner *Andrea Doria* sank 50 miles south of Nantucket after colliding in fog with the Swedish ship *Stockholm*; 52 were killed; 1,662 were rescued. Overall, losses have been reduced since 1914, when the Cape Cod Canal linked Cape Cod Bay with Buzzards Bay and allowed ships to avoid treacherous shoals. Today 30,000 ships and boats use the canal annually.

Lighthouses and Lifesaving

A major step in aiding ship-wreck victims was taken in 1872 when Congress established the U.S. Life Saving Service, a predecessor to today's Coast Guard. Nine stations were initially built at Monomoy, Chatham, Orleans, Nauset, Cahoon Hollow, Pamet River, Peaked Hill Bars, Highland, and Race Point. Eventually others joined them at Monomoy Point, Old Harbor, High Head, and Wood End. All were manned almost entirely by local men. From 1872 to 1915, station crews patrolled the beaches day and night in rain,

fog, and blizzard, meeting at halfway stations to exchange tokens and return to their stations. If a wreck or a ship in trouble was sighted, a red Coston flare was ignited to alert the ship that it had been seen. Then the station crew brought the 18-foot surfboat on a cart drawn by horse or by hand to the site. If the surf proved too rough to launch the boat, the crew attempted to shoot a life line from a small cannon to the stricken vessel, from which a "breeches buoy" could be suspended and the victims taken off one by one. In these pictures, a Life Sav-

ing Service crew poses at one of the Chatham stations and in a drill another crew gets ready to haul its surfboat by horse to the water. In the 43 years of its existence, the Cape's Life Saving Service performed hundreds of sea rescues, some of truly heroic proportions. Despite their motto—"You have to go, but you don't have to come back"—there was very little loss of life among the crews, a tribute to their skill and training. After the Cape Cod Canal was built in 1914, the number of shipwrecks de-

clined greatly. In 1915 the Life Saving stations were made a part of the newly-created U.S. Coast Guard. Today the Coast Guard staffs stations only at Provincetown, Chatham, Sandwich, and Woods Hole; the old Nauset station (shown in color) is now a part of the National Seashore. The recent advent of ship radar, radio beacons, LORAN, and other sophisticated navigational equipment has even further reduced the risks of offshore travel. Despite all these improvements, the sandbars and storms of the Outer Cape have not claimed their last victims.

ships and more than 100 men were lost on Georges Banks. Truro alone lost 57 men. When Thoreau passed through Truro a decade after the storm, the community was still in mourning: " 'Who lives in that house?' I inquired. 'Three widows,' was the reply."

The first organized attempt to aid shipwrecked sailors was made in 1794, when the Massachusetts Humane Society began to build a series of Humane Houses, or Charity Huts, along the Outer Beach. Located at the "hollows" in the sea cliff for ease of access, these Humane Houses were at first no more than crude huts, irregularly stocked with straw, matches, and a few other items of survival that might see a shipwrecked sailor through the night. Later they were equipped with small boats and rope lines with mortars that volunteer crews might use to try to reach sailors stranded offshore.

Cape Cod, or Highland, Light, the first lighthouse on the Cape, was erected in 1796 atop the clay cliffs in North Truro. In the next 70 years others followed: the twin lights of Chatham in 1808; Race Point in 1816; Monomoy in 1823; Long Point in 1826; the original "Three Sisters of Nauset" in 1838; and Wood End in 1872. The establishment of these lights significantly reduced the number of wrecks off the back shore. But lighthouses and beacons were of little help during intense fogs or furious northeast storms when anchors dragged and sailing ships caught rounding the Cape could not manage to stay offshore. More often than not ships became trapped between the outer and inner bars, and Cape residents had to stand helplessly on the shore as men froze in the rigging or were washed overboard into icy seas only a hundred yards from land.

A major step in aiding these wreck victims was taken in 1872, when Congress established the U.S. Life Saving Service, the culmination of a series of federal measures that had begun in 1847 with an appropriation to subsidize the Massachusetts Humane Society. Nine stations were initially built, and eventually four others joined them. In 1915 the U.S. Life Saving Service was merged with the Revenue Cutter Service to form the U.S. Coast Guard.

Ironically, the sea disasters provided yet one more way of making a living for Cape Codders. Compassionate and selfless as they were in their efforts to save lives and aid victims of wrecks wherever possible, they were also pragmatic. Salvaging, or wrecking, as it was called, provided windfalls for the local populace. This practice gave rise to the legend of the nefarious "mooncussers," men who deliberately lured ships to their doom with lighted lanterns on the beach on dark, moonless nights.

There is no evidence that "mooncussing" was ever engaged in by Cape Codders, but they were both philosophic and industrious about what the sea threw up on their shores, whether drift whales or freighters filled with useful cargo. During the 19th century wrecking became a true business. Salvaging crews were organized and hired by owners of wrecked ships to refloat or unload the vessels. Some local farmers spent as much time on the beaches as they did in their fields. E. Hayes Small of North Truro was one such man. On one occasion, using heavy block and tackle, cradles and eight horses, he hoisted 15,000 board feet of lumber off the beach to the top of the 150-foot bluffs north of Highland Light.

In 1914, however, a long-envisioned project finally became a reality and forever changed the history of wrecks, wrecking, and lifesaving on Cape Cod. A canal across the Cape, eliminating the entire arduous and dangerous outside passage for ships sailing between Boston and New York, had been dreamed of by Pilgrim leader Myles Standish, proposed as early as 1676, and approved in principle by George Washington. However, despite numerous government studies and the formation of at least four private canal companies, nothing substantial was accomplished until 1906, when New York financier Augustus P. Belmont took control of the Boston, New York, and Cape Cod Canal Company. Construction began on June 19, 1909, and the first vessels sailed through the newly completed Canal on July 29, 1914. The longest sea-level canal in the world, it was widened to 500 feet in 1935, and the present Sagamore and Bourne bridges were constructed. Today some 30,000 vessels annually sail through its protected passage.

With the canal's completion, the number of shipwrecks off the back side of the Cape declined precipitously, and so did the need for the 13 manned Life Saving stations. In 1915 they were incorporated into the newly-formed U.S. Coast Guard. Today the Outer Cape has only two Coast Guard stations, one at Chatham Light, the other in Provincetown Harbor.

Birds of the Shore

Red-breasted merganser

Lesser and greater yellowlegs

American oystercatcher

Ruddy turnstone

Canvasback pair

Ring-billed gull

Sanderlings

Osprey

Dunlin

Snowy egret

Common terns

Spotted sandpiper

Great blue heron

Green-backed heron

Willet

Common eider family

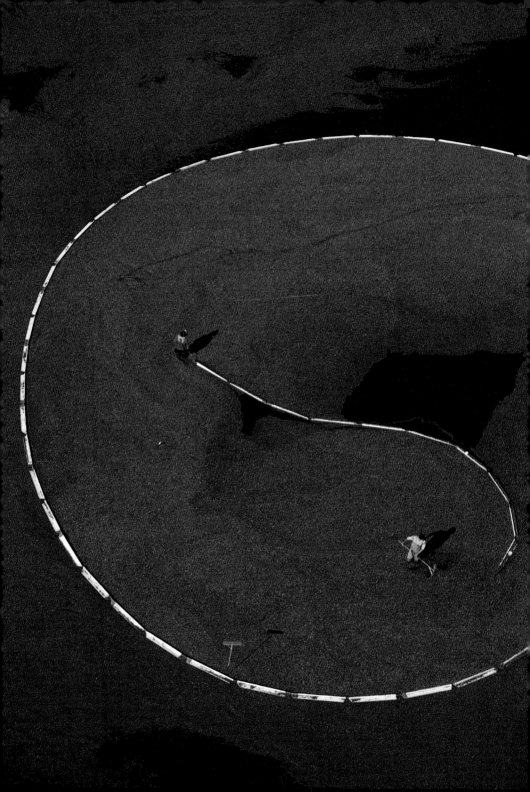

The Cape's Transformation

The Cape Cod that Thoreau visited nearly a century and a half ago was a rural, semi-isolated peninsula with a distinct maritime culture. Villages were small; most food and materials were obtained locally; travel by land over sand roads was slow and difficult; and, although many a local shipmaster had visited Singapore and São Paulo, most native Cape Codders spent their lives within a few miles of their birthplace, except when they went to sea to fish. Language was local, not only in its flat Cape accent, but in a host of names and phrases attached to local plants, animals, and weather.

Off-Cape visitors were rare and often regarded with suspicion. Thoreau and his traveling companion, William Ellery Channing, were initially mistaken for bank robbers. Though a steamboat ran regularly from Boston to Provincetown, travel elsewhere on the peninsula was still difficult. Aside from a few hardy, curious souls like Thoreau, the only regular summer visitors to the Cape in the mid-19th century were those attending the Methodist camp-meetings, such as the one described by him at Millennium Grove in Eastham. "At present," he said of Cape Cod, "it is wholly unknown to the fashionable world." Yet Thoreau was perceptive enough to realize that "The time must come when this coast will be a place of resort for those New Englanders who really wish to visit the seaside"—though even he could not have imagined how complete that transformation would be.

After the Civil War, the Cape entered a period of economic decline that lasted for more than half a century. With the decline of the merchant marine, whaling, and fishing fleets, and the opening up of the rich western prairies, many of the Cape's younger people left to seek their fortune elsewhere. Hundreds of acres of farmland were abandoned. The Cape's population, which reached a high of 35,990 in 1860, reached a low of 26,670 in 1920. Wellfleet lost 65 percent of its population, and Truro nearly 75 percent.

CAPE COD B. RAILROAD.
Summer Arrangement.

In 1851 trains ran in the summer between Boston and Sandwich. The fare was $1.50, one way.

Ironically, it was the railroad—which initially contributed to the decline in the packet boat and merchant marine trade—that subsequently helped revive the Cape's economy. The Cape Cod Branch Railroad first arrived at Sandwich in 1848. Rails were gradually extended down-Cape, finally reaching Provincetown in 1873. The completed railroad linked Cape towns to the rest of New England and made inland resources such as coal and lumber widely available. More importantly, for the first time the Cape itself became accessible to the region's urban population.

Oddly enough, the first railroad advertisements enticed Cape Codders to Boston, rather than the reverse. But it was not long before the "fashionable world" began to discover the charms of Cape Cod. "Summer folk," including President Grover Cleveland, began building substantial homes with imported lumber along the shores of Buzzards Bay, Nantucket Sound, and Pleasant Bay.

Bird shooting became a popular sport on the Cape, and several gunning clubs were established for vacationing sportsmen from Boston and New York. These clubs, combined with the commercial hunting of waterfowl and shorebirds for the food market and millinery trade, took a tremendous toll on the Cape's bird populations from the Civil War until the passage of the Federal Migratory Bird Treaties of 1916. According to one report, 8,000 golden plovers and Eskimo curlews were shot on the Cape in one day! (The former species is now a rare migrant, the latter presumed extinct.) At the same time, much of the most valuable shorebird habitat was being destroyed. Hundreds of acres of salt marshes were dredged to expand harbors or filled in for development, agriculture, and mosquito control.

A different kind of transformation began in Provincetown in 1899, when Charles Hawthorne opened his Cape Cod School of Art, officially initiating the emergence of the Cape-tip as a major art colony. By 1916 there were five art schools operating in Provincetown. That year also saw the formation of the Provincetown Players, one of the most important small theaters in the history of American drama. Its founders—which included George Cram "Jig" Cook, playwright Susan Glaspell, and author Mary Heaton Vorse—produced original plays in a shack on a harbor wharf, plays that included the early works of a then-unknown dramatist, Eugene O'Neill.

Since then the towns of the Outer Cape have been seasonal and year-round homes to a host of artistic and literary figures. Edward Hopper, Edwin Dickinson, Karl Knaths, Ross Moffett, Henry Hensche, Hans Hoffman, Ben Shahn, Mark Rothko, Jackson Pollack, Robert Motherwell, Alice Stallknecht, and Arnold Geissbuhler are a few of the influential painters and sculptors who have worked and lived on the Outer Cape. Literary figures have included John Reed, William Daniel Steele, John Dos Passos, Edmund Wilson, Edna St. Vincent Millay, Mary McCarthy, Elizabeth Bishop, Provincetown's "Poet of the Dunes" Harry Kemp, Norman Mailer, Howard Nemerov, Alan Dugan, Stanley Kunitz, Marge Piercy, and Annie Dillard.

A particularly rich vein of the Cape's creative activity has been the literary treatment of the landscape itself. Thoreau's *Cape Cod* (1864) was the first recognized classic of this genre. Others have included *The Outermost House* by Henry Beston, *The House on Nauset Marsh* by Dr. Wyman Richardson, *The Great Beach* by Brewster author John Hay, and the poetry of Provincetown's Pulitzer-Prize winner Mary Oliver.

Walter Smith, 1849-1932, retired in 1930 as at least the seventh in a long line of town criers that lasted into the late 1980s in Provincetown. Traditionally they gave out news of village events, antiques sales, church suppers, and the like. For a fee, they also advertised products for local merchants.

After World War I the first paved roads were constructed down-Cape. With the arrival of the automobile, the second wave of the Cape's transformation began. The weekender appeared. Cottage colonies began to spring up in the towns and on the beaches. Golf courses were built, including the Highland Links in Truro and the Nauset Links in Eastham. The Nauset Links fairways today are a cedar forest through which the visitor can walk on the Seashore's Nauset Marsh Trail.

The Cape's summer population began to mushroom, and Provincetown in particular took on a distinctively Bohemian ambience during the 1920s and 1930s. At the same time, the descendants of the Portuguese immigrants came to dominate Provincetown's fishing fleet. Even today nearly a third of its permanent population claims Portuguese descent and continues to give a distinctive Old World flavor to this community's cuisine, culture, and local festivals.

Having lived with change throughout their history,

Two Henrys: Thoreau and Beston

Cape Cod has attracted a number of authors who have written countless stories and books about the place. Two books that have become classics were written by Henry David Thoreau and by Henry Beston. Thoreau's *Cape Cod* was published posthumously in 1865 and tells of visits totaling 3 weeks that he made to the Cape in 1849, 1850, and 1855. He walked to Provincetown from Eastham absorbing its geologic and natural history and observing the solitary life of its people, especially the lighthouse keepers and shipwreck scavengers, known as

"wreckers." Thoreau may have been the first in print to liken the Cape to a "bared and bended arm of Massachusetts." He was especially fascinated with the beach from Nauset Harbor to Race Point and with the bluff abruptly rising to its west. "This sandbank—the backbone of the Cape—rose directly from the beach to the height of a hundred feet or more above the ocean. It was with singular emotions that we first stood upon it and discovered what a place we had chosen to walk on. . . . a perfect desert of shining sand. . . ." In his day more of

the Cape was barren than today, but efforts to plant grasses were already underway. Henry Beston spent more time on the Cape than Thoreau, and he stayed mostly in one place. His book, *The Outermost House*, tells of a year, in 1927-28, he spent among the elements at a 2-room, 10-windowed cottage in the dunes on Nauset Beach opposite Fort Hill in Eastham (background photo). As Thoreau had done at Walden Pond, Beston chronicled nature's seasonal sights, sounds, and smells on this narrow spit of sand, a place of "outermost" exposure. "Listen to the surf,

Henry David Thoreau

Henry Beston

really lend it your ears," Beston wrote, "and you will hear in it a world of sounds: hollow boomings and heavy roarings, great watery tumblings and tramplings, long hissing seethes, sharp rifle-shot reports, splashes, whispers, the grinding undertone of stones, and sometimes vocal sounds that might be the half-heard talk of people in the sea." Beston's cottage became a National Literary Landmark in 1964, but in 1978 it was washed away in a storm. No doubt he would have assented to what the elements had done.

The Cranberry Bog

Cranberries are among the true natives of Cape Cod. The plant, *Vaccinium macrocarpon*, is a low evergreen shrub of the heath family that grows in bogs. Legend has it that the plant originally was named craneberry because its small, bell-shaped, pink flowers look like the neck and head of a crane, or heron, that stalks marshes and bogs. The deep red, nearly round, acidic berry is almost a half-inch in diameter. Indians called cranberries sassamanesh. They used this fruit as food and medicine; they mixed ripe berries with dried venison to make pemmican and placed roasted unripe berries on wounds. They also taught Pilgrims to use wild cranberries in their foods, and the colonists shipped 10 barrels of them to Charles II, but he found them too tart. Cranberries remained popular on the Cape, however, and by 1773 anyone caught picking more than a quart in Province-town before September 20 would be fined a dollar—and would have to surrender the berries. Sailing ships served cranberries to their crews to prevent or cure scurvy. In 1813 Henry Hall of North Dennis made a discovery that led to commercial production: the berries became invigorated when sand drifted on the plants.

Soon other Cape Codders were purposely sanding their bogs, and production was rising. By 1855 Cape Cod was a major Massachusetts producer with 2,408 acres in cranberries. Today about 1,250 acres are in production, 10 percent of the state's total. Besides needing bogs with good peat bottoms, growers must have a water supply for sprinklers or enough water to flood their bogs through a series of ditches. Between November and March, and occasionally at other times, bogs are flooded to prevent frost from killing the vines. Ice up to 8 inches thick is allowed to form and the water below it is drained off. To sand the bogs, the ice is covered every 3 to 5 years with up to an inch of sand, which sinks to the bottom when the ice melts. In April the meltwater is drained off. Harvesting starts in September and continues through October. In this old postcard (below), pickers armed with wooden-toothed scoops move across a bog harvesting the berries. Today the process has been mechanized. More than 100 cranberry varieties have been developed, but the Early Black and

Howes are direct descendants of the wild ones growing on the Cape. Processors now produce sauces, juices, and relishes that have become as closely associated with Thanksgiving as the Pilgrims and turkeys.

As the number of summer visitors increased, inns and cottages such as these in Wellfleet were built to take in lodgers. In 1911, Provincetown's Commercial Street, right, had restaurants, lodgings, ice cream shops, and other facilities for tourists arriving by car as well as by boat.

Cape Codders adjusted to these outside influences with philosophy and pragmatism. As Cape historian Henry Kittredge observed in 1930: "If whales no longer visit their shores, rich city folk do, and with easy adaptability Cape men and women take the goods the gods provide them." Some local residents began to rent out rooms in their old Cape houses, while others added on a front porch for a restaurant, set up a gas station or a beach plum jelly stand in the front yard, or an antiques store in the barn. Some took advantage of less legal commerce of the era; during Prohibition a number of trawler captains turned to the more lucrative sea-trade of rum-running.

At least one native industry survived, in fact flourished, during these years of decline and transformation. Cranberries had been commercially raised on the Cape's bogs since the early 1800s, but the coming of the railroad opened off-Cape markets for the crop. The cranberry, as much as the cod, became the symbol of Cape Cod. In recent years, because of the success of modern marketing, many small bogs that were abandoned over the last half century have been put back into cultivation. One of these old bogs, established by James Howe in the 1880s on North Pamet Road in Truro, has been partially restored by the National Park Service.

The third and unquestionably the most sweeping transformation of the Cape's culture and landscape has occurred since World War II. With the building of the Mid-Cape Highway and the expansion of the post-war economy, the first waves of modern "washashores," or permanent immigrants, began to arrive over the Bourne and Sagamore bridges. From 1940 to 1990 the Cape's year-round population increased from about 30,000 to more than 175,000, with a summertime population that swells to 500,000 or more. Each year from 1970 to 1990 an average of 5,000 acres (roughly the size of Provincetown) was developed for residential and commercial uses.

Though the Cape has been technically an island since 1914, it continues to be increasingly a part of the mainland. The old, indigenous, rural maritime culture of the Cape is irretrievably gone, though small fishing fleets continue to go out of local harbors and inlets. Cape Codders now live in a cosmopolitan contemporary culture, sharing more with their urban counterparts than with the sea

In these days of instant world-wide communications via satellites, it is difficult to imagine the excitement that came with the advent of wireless telegraphy and radio. In the 1890s, the idea of transmitting long-distance messages via electromagnetic waves captured the imagination of Guglielmo Marconi, a young Italian. In 1899 Marconi succeeded in sending a radio message across the English Channel, and, he went to work on developing a transatlantic system. Two communications cables already had been laid on the bottom of the ocean between France and

Guglielmo Marconi displays his wireless telegraphy equipment in England in 1896. The Leyden jar capacitor and boxlike transformer (below) *represent an application of Marconi's invention in World War I for national defense, maritime safety, and commercial communications.*

Cape Cod. Marconi, too, selected a site for a station on the Cape, high on a cliff overlooking the ocean in South Wellfleet. He built others at Glace Bay, Nova Scotia, and at Poldhu in Great Britain. At first the antennas at South Wellfleet and Poldhu consisted of huge rings of masts, but these were destroyed by gales before any messages could be transmitted. They were replaced at each place by 4 towers 210 feet high. In December 1901, at an experimental site in St. John's, Newfoundland, Marconi received the first transatlantic signal, 3 dots for the letter "S," from Britain. In December 1902 his Glace Bay station received a complete message from Poldhu. On the night of January 18, 1903, he transmitted from South Wellfleet this message, in Morse code, from President Theodore Roosevelt to King Edward VII: "In taking advantage of the wonderful triumph of scientific research and ingenuity which has been achieved in perfecting a system of wireless telegraphy, I extend on behalf of the American people most cordial greetings and good wishes to you and to all the people of the British Empire." The king replied in a similar vein, making this the first 2-way wireless communication between Europe and America. Soon newspapers and others were transmitting messages across the Atlantic, and the wireless became the common way of communicating with ships. For 15 years telegraphers sent out messages on the South Wellfleet spark-gap transmitter. But in 1917 the Navy closed the station. It was dismantled in 1920 and scrapped. Its successor, WCC in Chatham, operated until 1993.

At South Wellfleet Marconi first built a circular antenna consisting of 20 ship masts 200 feet high about 165 feet back from the edge of the ridge overlooking the Atlantic. The masts were blown down in a storm November 25, 1901.

This ironstone plate commemorates the first wireless message, received from President Theodore Roosevelt by King Edward VII on January 19, 1903, and shows the 4 towers that replaced the 20 masts.

MARCONI WIRELESS STATION, WELLFLEET, MASS.
THE FIRST WIRELESS MESSAGE FROM
PRESIDENT ROOSEVELT to KING EDWARD VII
WAS SENT FROM THIS STATION
JAN 19TH 1903.

captains in whose 200-year-old houses they may dwell or spend the night.

With this staggering growth and its resultant pressures on the Cape's resources and natural habitats, there has been an increasing movement to protect the Cape's fragile landscape and its wildlife. The most dramatic and sweeping manifestation of this was the Congressional authorization of the Cape Cod National Seashore itself in 1961, but a number of homegrown environmental research, conservation, and educational organizations have also been established. These groups include the Center for Coastal Studies in Provincetown, the Wellfleet Bay Audubon Sanctuary, the Cape Cod Museum of Natural History in Brewster, the Association for the Preservation of Cape Cod, and the Compact of Cape Cod Conservation Trusts.

In part because of the work of these and other groups, general environmental awareness has also grown. The Cape's salt marshes are no longer regarded as wasteland to be dredged for marinas or filled for development but as one of the richest and most productive marine habitats in the world. Local kettle pond shores, once built up with little regard for environmental impact, are now recognized as important buffers protecting water quality and as important habitat for certain flowering plants, some of which are found in only a handful of sites worldwide.

No longer are local whales driven ashore or hunted with harpoons. Instead, today's Cape Codders ply a lucrative trade running whale-watching trips out of Provincetown and other ports, and a Cape Cod Stranding Network has been established to aid stranded whales and other marine animals.

Shorebirds, too, have ceased to be slaughtered by the thousands on our beaches and in our marshes. Instead, areas such as the Monomoy Wildlife Refuge and the National Seashore provide protected feeding and resting stations for thousands of migrating shorebirds and waterfowl. Each summer sections of beaches and dunes within the Seashore and elsewhere are roped off and patrolled to insure the survival of such local nesting species as terns and piping plovers, and park talks and walks stress to visitors the importance and fragility of these breeding areas.

Besides changes in human attitudes and practice, natural changes in wildlife populations continue to take place as well. As ocean waters warm, cold-water species such as cod and halibut have moved farther north, while warmer-water species such as striped bass and bluefish seem to be increasing. Sizable numbers of wintering harbor seals have appeared in the Cape's estuaries and offshore beaches in the past 20 years, and during the winter of 1989-90, for the first time ever, some rare gray seals gave birth to several pups on Monomoy Island. Willets and oyster-catchers, after a long absence, are nesting on Cape beaches once again, and ospreys, responding to artificial nesting platforms, have returned to Cape bays and ponds after their disappearance during the 1960s from DDT poisoning. Other recent self-arrivals on the Cape's wildlife scene include opossums, house finches, and even coyotes.

What do all these changes and transformations teach us? It may be, most importantly, that we still confront what the First Comers faced: the land itself, sea-born and sea-shaped. When we learn its history and observe the age-old forces that continue to work today, the lesson seems to be that any human occu-pation of the Earth is, at best, tentative and transi-tory, and particularly so here. The waves, beaches, dunes, and trees of the Cape continue to dance, and we have begun to learn to dance with them—to understand and adapt to the land's rhythms, tempos, and limits—so that we and those who come after us may continue to enjoy all that it has to offer. For it is we, residents and visitors alike, who are today's Cape Codders.

Wildflowers

White water lily

Seaside goldenrod

Pink ladyslipper

Beach plum

Dewberry

St. Johnswort

Purple aster

Sheep laurel

82

Bittersweet nightshade

Beach heather, or poverty grass

Prickly pear cactus

Beach-pea

Creeping bellflower

Canada mayflower

Star-flower

Cypress spurge

Part 3

Guide and Adviser

Though Cape Cod has been known as Massachusetts' major summer resort for many years, it is now attracting a number of travelers at all times of the year. Today more than 5 million people visit the Cape annually.

Those wishing to avoid crowds may prefer to walk its windswept beaches and tour its historic sites between September and June, the off-season.

That's tip Number 1 in this handbook's Guide and Adviser section, which focuses on that part of Cape Cod containing the National Seashore. This is the area, known as the Lower or Outer Cape, between Chatham and Provincetown. Some information also is provided to help you travel throughout the rest of Cape Cod and neighboring offshore islands. The first few pages deal with general travel tips and activities information. Then, 2-page spreads take closer looks at towns within or near the 27,000-acre National Seashore. They are followed by travel tips about nearby Cape Cod attractions and the islands of Martha's Vineyard and Nantucket.

Seasons

The summer beach season in July and August attracts the most vacationers, especially families with children. But enough tourist facilities are open in the fall, winter, and spring to take care of lodging and food needs.

In July and August daytime temperatures usually rise into the 80s°F. From September through November, temperatures gradually decline from the 70s to the 50s, or lower. Fall's cool, brisk days make the Cape a favorite destination for some New Englanders on the Columbus Day and Thanksgiving holidays.

Winters are generally cold and windy, with temperatures averaging in the 30s during the day and in the 20s at night. The Atlantic Ocean and Cape Cod

Bay help to moderate the winter temperatures, so the Cape's snowfall is considerably less than the mainland's.

As in all parts of New England, spring is short, arriving at the earliest in April and often not until June. Like the fall, however, spring can be one of the most pleasant times on Cape Cod because of the relative solitude.

Transportation

Major highways leading to Cape Cod are I-495 and Mass. 3 from the Boston area and I-195 from Providence, R.I., and Fall River, Mass. On the Cape itself U.S. 6 is the primary road to and through the National Seashore. Those wishing to travel through the Mid-Cape, or Upper Cape, towns and villages may use Mass. 6A on the north side or Mass. 28 on the south. In the summer, traffic moves slowly on most roads and highways.

Buses Major bus lines serve Hyannis on the Cape from Boston, Providence, Fall River, and New Bedford. Additional routes run from Hyannis to Chatham and Provincetown.

Air Service Flights operate from Boston, Providence, and New York City to Hyannis and between Boston and Provincetown. Private and charter planes may use airstrips in Hyannis, Chatham, and Provincetown.

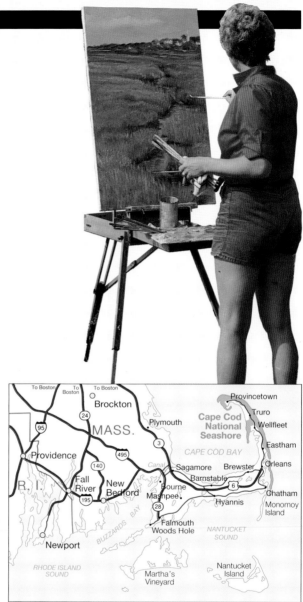

Ferries A passengers-only ferry runs in summer between Boston and Provincetown. Passenger and vehicle ferries operate from Woods Hole and Hyannis to Martha's Vineyard and Nantucket in the summer. Ferry services to the islands are limited in other seasons. For further information: Woods Hole, Martha's Vineyard & Nantucket Steamship Authority, P.O. Box 284, Dept. CG, Woods Hole, MA 02543-0284, telephone 508-540-2022; or Hy-line Cruises, Ocean Street Dock, Pier #1, Hyannis, MA 02601-4715, telephone 508-778-2600.

Cape Cod National Seashore

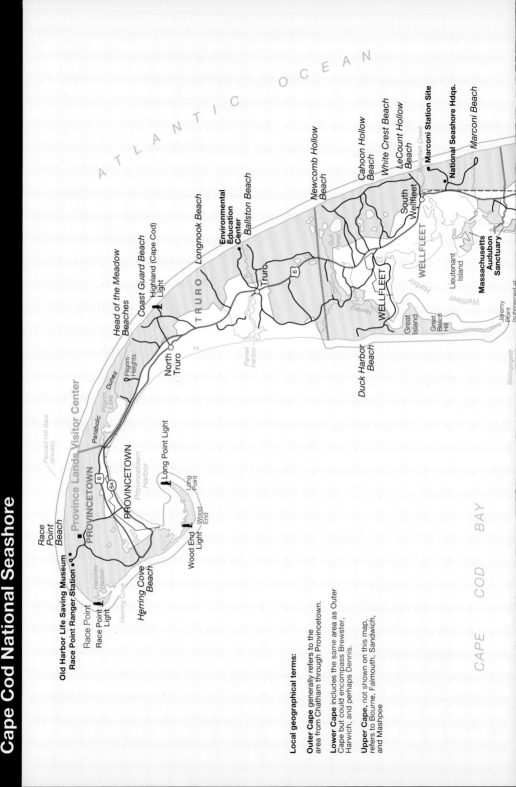

ATLANTIC OCEAN

Race Point Beach

Peaked Hill Bars (shoals)

Old Harbor Life Saving Museum
Race Point Ranger Station

Province Lands Visitor Center

PROVINCETOWN

Race Point
Race Point Light

Hatches Harbor

Herring Cove

Herring Cove Beach

PROVINCETOWN

Provincetown Harbor

6
6A

Long Point Light

Long Point

Wood End

Wood End Light

Parabolic Dunes

Pilgrim Lake

Pilgrim Heights

North Truro

Head of the Meadow Beaches

Coast Guard Beach

Highland (Cape Cod) Light

Longnook Beach

TRURO

Environmental Education Center

Ballston Beach

Pamet Harbor

Truro

6

Pamet River

Newcomb Hollow Beach

Cahoon Hollow Beach

White Crest Beach

LeCount Hollow Beach

Blackfish Creek

Marconi Station Site

National Seashore Hdqs.

Marconi Beach

South Wellfleet

WELLFLEET

Gull Pond

Herring River

Duck Harbor Beach

Great Island

Great Beach Hill

WELLFLEET

Wellfleet Harbor

Lieutenant Island

Massachusetts Audubon Sanctuary

Jeremy Point

Billingsgate

CAPE COD BAY

Local geographical terms:

Outer Cape generally refers to the area from Chatham through Provincetown.

Lower Cape includes the same area as Outer Cape but could encompass Brewster, Harwich, and perhaps Dennis.

Upper Cape, not shown on this map, refers to Bourne, Falmouth, Sandwich, and Mashpee.

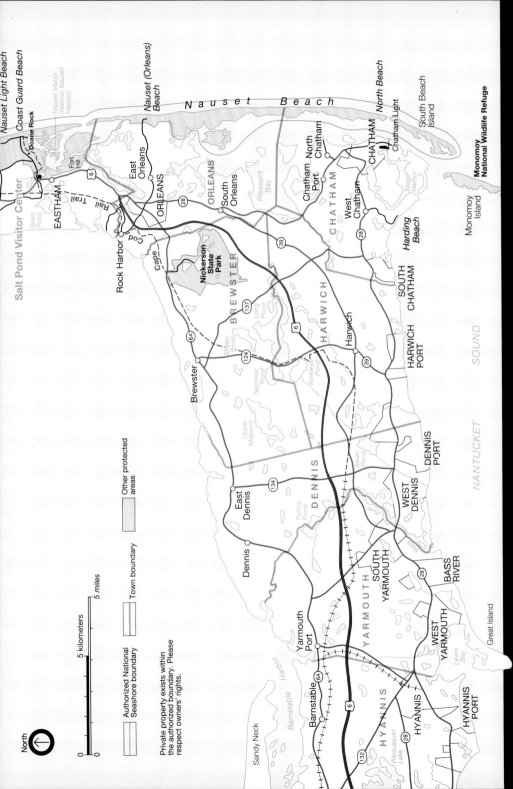

The National Park Service operates two major visitor centers in Cape Cod National Seashore.

The **Salt Pond Visitor Center** on U.S. 6 in Eastham has an information desk, exhibits on the natural and human history of the Cape, audiovisual shows, a bookstore, and special programs. A foot trail from the center goes by Nauset Marsh; the bike path leads to the beach. The Buttonbush Trail, with special features for the blind, is located next to the visitor center parking lot. Ask about other facilities and services accessible to those with disabilities.

The **Province Lands Visitor Center** in Provincetown is smaller than the one at Salt Pond, but it offers similar services. Exhibits and guided walks focus on the life of the dunes.

Both visitor centers are open daily from spring until late fall, and the staffs at both centers offer guided walks, talks, and evening programs on the Cape's natural and human history. The many subjects include life of the marshes, seashore ecology, geology, archeology, birdlife, Indians, early settlers, and ar-chitecture. These services are provided daily in the summer and on a reduced basis in the spring and from Labor Day through Columbus Day. Ask for schedules at the visitor centers.

The **Race Point Ranger Station** in Provincetown provides year-round informational services. Informational services also are available in the winter at the Salt Pond Visitor Center and at park headquarters in South Wellfleet.

Environmental Education
The National Seashore is host to 2 environmental education centers that accommodate educational groups on an advanced booking basis during the school year. For further information, write to the National Seashore.

Camping

There are no campgrounds operated by the National Park Service, but a number of private commercial campgrounds are located within the boundaries of the National Seashore. Otherwise camping on park lands is prohibited. The Roland C. Nickerson State Park, on Mass. 6A in nearby Brewster, offers camping on a first-come, first-served basis from mid-April to mid-October; there are no trailer hookups. The park address is Main Street, Brewster, MA 02631-0003, and the telephone number is 508-896-3491. For information about private campgrounds, write or telephone the Cape Cod Chamber of Commerce (see below).

The National Seashore is a place of discovery, a place to find bird tracks, horseshoe crabs, shells, polished stones, and life along trails.

Travel Services

Restaurants, hotels, motels, gifts shops, stores, gasoline stations, and other facilities are located in nearby towns and villages. Lodging reservations are essential in July and August. For information and to make reservations, write: Cape Cod Chamber of Commerce, Routes 6 and 132, Hyannis, MA 02601-0016; or telephone: 508-362-3225.

Further Information

For specific inquiries about the Seashore prior to or after a visit, write: Superintendent, Cape Cod National Seashore, 99 Marconi Site Road, Wellfleet, MA 02667; or telephone 508-349-3785. Call the Salt Pond Visitor Center at 508-255-3421, or the Province Lands Visitor Center (closed in winter) at 508-487-1256.

Coast Guard Beach

The Cape's recreational activities are mostly water-related, naturally. Its many beaches, harbors, and inlets offer endless opportunities whether you want to swim, surf, sail, fish, water-ski, use a motorboat, or just sunbathe.

Swimming

Within the National Seashore, lifeguard services, restrooms, changing areas, and related facilities are located at these beaches operated by the National Park Service from Eastham to Provincetown: Coast Guard, Nauset Light, Marconi, Head of the Meadow, Race Point, and Herring Cove (see map on pages 88-89). Several towns also have public beaches; all of them charge parking fees in the summer.

The water usually is quite cold—temperatures may be in the high 50s °F even in the summer—and the surf can be rough

at times, so be especially careful. Some parents with young children prefer beaches on Cape Cod Bay to those on the Atlantic coast because the water is warmer and usually calmer and because the beaches slope more gradually into the water. See rip current warning, page 108.

Motorboating

The many inlets and harbors along the coastlines make the Cape appealing to motorboaters. Most town harbors have boat launching ramps, boat rentals, and other facilities. Marine supply stores are located in most Cape towns.

Some harbors, such as Provincetown, Wellfleet, Orleans, Chatham, Harwich Port, and Woods Hole, have docks, moorings, and other marine facilities for those visiting the Cape by powerboat. Write to the Chamber of Commerce or inquire locally for specific information.

Sailing, Surfing, and Windsurfing

Sailboats and sailboards are a familiar sight in Cape Cod waters from Buzzards Bay and Nantucket Sound to the Atlantic itself and Cape Cod Bay. In the National Seashore area, bays and harbors in Chatham, Orleans, Wellfleet, and Provincetown are excellent for those using small sailboats and sailboards. The Atlantic coast from Orleans to Provincetown is usually good for surfboarding. Special areas are designated for their use at beaches run by the National Park Service. If in doubt, inquire locally.

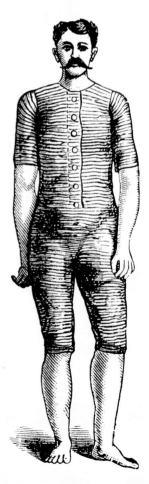

Fishing

Saltwater fishing is one of the most popular recreational activities on the Cape. Surf-fishermen line up on the more accessible beaches to cast their lines into the Atlantic for striped bass, bluefish, and flounder, while others seek secluded spots to try their luck.

Charter fishing boats work out of Chatham, Orleans, Wellfleet, and Provincetown. Besides the fish cited above, you might catch halibut, haddock, and mackerel.

No license is required for saltwater sport fishing, but there are size and number limits and a state license is necessary for fishing in the many freshwater ponds. Commercial fishing is not permitted within the National Seashore. Inquire at town offices or fishing supply stores about regulations and for other information.

Shellfishing

Because so many clams and other shellfish have been harvested for so many years, the supplies are dwindling and towns regulate their gathering and areas and times when shellfishing is allowed. You must obtain a town shellfish permit.

While on the Cape, you will hear about "mussels," "steamers," "quahogs," and "little necks." What are the differences?

Mussels, which are dark blue oblongs about 2½ inches long, are found in groups attached to rocks or pilings.

Mussels

Surf casting at Race Point, Provincetown

Quahogs are grayish hardshell clams that are commonly used in chowders. Small quahogs, known as little necks or cherrystones, are served raw. Quahogs are dug with a widetoothed rake, or scratcher, primarily along the Cape Cod Bay shoreline at low tide and in the shallows of Nauset Bay and Pleasant Bay. From their boats, commercial shellfishermen use a heavy, long-handled rake that looks like a wire basket on the end of two long poles.

Quahog

Softshells are whitish, oblong clams that are steamed or fried. They are dug with a small finetoothed rake, or clam hoe, at low tide on sand flats facing the Atlantic, Nantucket Sound, and Cape Cod Bay. You can spot their locations by tiny holes in the sand. Sometimes they squirt water at you as you step near their holes.

Softshell clam

Other common shellfish are bay or sea **scallops.** Scallop shells come in a variety of colors and have ribs or elevated ridges running from the top to the outer edges. Bay scallops usually are found in eelgrass beds.

A tip to out-of-staters: Cape Cod clam chowder is made with a milk base. Manhattan clam chower is made with a tomato base. Do not expect the latter on the Cape. Don't even ask for it!

Humans trace their ancestry to animals that left the sea and moved onto land. Whales trace their ancestry to a group of mammals that left the land 60 million years ago and returned to the sea. In relatively more recent times, Cape Cod, Nantucket, and New Bedford were East Coast centers for the harvesting of whales. Today, the Cape is a major center for the watching of whales. Commercial sightseeing boats conduct whale-watching tours of 3 to 8 hours from piers in Provincetown, Barnstable, and Plymouth from April to November. In the spring whales can be seen off the Cape migrating from the south, and in the fall they can be seen migrating from the north. Whales commonly seen off the Cape include the humpback, minke, and finback. Right

Minke whale
Spouts rarely seen; sleek, like finback, but much smaller; body gray above, light underside; white band on flippers; narrow, pointed head; 15 to 35 feet long; seen in spring and fall.

Right whale
V-shaped double spout; white callosities on head; short, rounded flippers; body black above and below, with white patches by chin and navel; no dorsal fin; shows black tail flukes when diving; 35 to 56 feet long; seen most often in spring.

whales are sometimes seen in the fall and spring. Whales may often be seen from land at Province Lands Visitor Center and from Race Point Beach. But you will see the whales up closer from a boat—and they will get a chance to watch you.

Humpback whale
Mushroom-shaped spout; long, white flippers; barnacles on snout; body black above, splotches of white on belly; very acrobatic, jumping, spinning, slapping tail; shows white patches on flukes when diving; 30 to 56 feet long; seen in spring and early summer.

Finback whale
Tall, slender spout; flat, wedge-shaped head; dark gray above white belly; left side dark gray, right side including lower jaw white like belly; gray stripes behind eyes forming V's on back; prominent dorsal fin; rarely shows tail when diving; 40 to 85 feet long; seen in spring, summer, and fall.

Biking in the Province Lands

Recreational opportunities abound on land as well as on or in the water. The National Seashore offers a number of short trails, a major biking trail, bridle paths, and birds, birds, birds.

Biking

The 26-mile Cape Cod Rail Trail follows an old railroad bed from Dennis to South Wellfleet. This trail connects the National Seashore with Nickerson State Park's camping facilities in Brewster.

Three bike trails are located within the National Seashore. The **Nauset Trail**, 1.6 miles long, starts at the Salt Pond Visitor Center and runs to Coast Guard Beach.

The **Head of the Meadow Trail** is 2 miles long and runs between High Head Road and Head of the Meadow Beach parking area in Truro. The trail commemorates the Pilgrims' first discovery of fresh drinking water in 1620.

The most difficult of the 3 trails is a **5¼-mile loop** through the dunes of the Province Lands area. A 1-mile spur from the loop leads to Herring Cove Beach on Cape Cod Bay. A half-mile spur leads to Race Point Beach.

Bikers may also take a roundtrip along the Cape Cod Canal.

Bicycles may be rented in Orleans, Eastham, and Provincetown.

Safety Tips   Check your brakes, gears, and steering before starting out, especially if you are using an unfamiliar bicycle. Wear a helmet.

All trails are two-way, so keep to the right.

Be alert for hikers and watch out for sand on the trails.

Use front and rear brakes together, or you may be thrown over the handlebars.

Do not speed.

Hiking

Walking the self-guiding trails located throughout the National Seashore is an excellent way to get away from the hurly-burly pace of the tourist areas and to get a sense of the Cape's natural and human history. Most of the trails are not arduous.

The **Nauset Marsh Trail** in Eastham is a 1-mile loop that starts at Salt Pond, a glacial kettle pond that is fed twice daily by the ocean. From the trail you can get a close look at the life of Nauset Marsh, which was a bay when Champlain explored the area in 1605.

The **Beech Forest Trail** on Race Point Road near the Province Lands Visitor Center consists of 2 loops totaling 1 mile and tells the story of dune ponds and the elimination of early forests of beech, oak, pine, and cedar on the Lower Cape.

The **Atlantic White Cedar Swamp Trail** of 1.2 miles starts at the Marconi Station Site in Wellfleet, descends inland through a landscape in which the trees gradually grow taller as the effects of the sea lessen. The trail ends at a white cedar swamp in a glacial kettle, and returns to the parking area on the Old Wireless Road.

For information on other trails, see pages 100-105. While hiking on the Cape, be on the watch for ticks (see Lyme disease precautions on page 108).

Red Maple Swamp Trail

Horseback Riding

Because of the fragility of the plants and soil, horseback riding is restricted to three bridle paths located in the Provincetown area and on designated dirt roads. Horses are not permitted on nature trails.

The **Sunset Trail** starts near Race Point Road and leads through dunes to the ocean. The **West Trail** starts at the same point but passes through shady pitch pine and black oak forests and by freshwater ponds and cranberry bogs. The **Herring Cove Trail** traverses a narrow barrier beach along Cape Cod Bay.

Allow 2 hours for a round trip on each of the bridle paths. Ask for more information about these trails at the visitor centers.

97

Birdwatching

Cape Cod is one of the best places for birdwatching on the East Coast. Besides the terns, gulls, and ducks common to most seashores, the Cape is a seasonal home to a great number of marsh and lowland dwellers and a stopover for numerous migratory species traveling the Atlantic Flyway. More than 360 species have been recorded.

Black duck

Some of the best places on the Lower Cape for birdwatching include Fort Hill, Coast Guard Beach, and Nauset Marsh in Eastham, the heathlands near Marconi Station, the Massachusetts Audubon Society's Wellfleet Bay Wildlife Sanctuary in South Wellfleet, the Pleasant Bay area and the Monomoy National Wildlife Refuge in Chatham, and, of course, all the beaches in between.

Clapper rail

With the right weather conditions, the Beech Forest in Provincetown is good for seeing spring migrants. Also in the spring, migrating hawks may be seen from many vantage points, and autumn falcon flights on Cape Cod can be spectacular. Watch for seabirds from Race Point Beach any time of the year but particularly after northeast winds.

Ask at the National Seashore visitor centers about checklists and other birding publications.

Belted kingfisher

Piping Plover, a Threatened Species

All birds are protected within the National Seashore, but the piping plover is getting special protection. This small, sand-colored bird once was commonly seen along the Atlantic Coast, but its numbers dwindled greatly because of habitat loss. In 1918 the piping plover came under the protection of the Migratory Bird Treaty. Its numbers rose until the 1940s, when increases in beach recreation and development again threatened the bird. In 1986 the piping plover was listed by the Federal Government as a threatened species.

The National Park Service and the U.S. Fish and Wildlife Service are jointly making efforts to protect piping plover nesting areas on the outer beaches. As a result, the piping plover's U.S. Atlantic coast population now totals nearly 1,000 pairs.

To help protect this threatened species, respect all areas fenced or posted, stay away from the birds and their nests, keep pets leashed on beaches where they are allowed, and do not bury any garbage on beaches, because it attracts predators.

Chatham fishing wharf

On the Outer Cape in the summer, the towns of Orleans, Brewster, and Chatham provide a full range of food, lodging, and other services and facilities for vacationers. Some facilities remain open year round.

The National Seashore's authorized boundaries encompass parts of Orleans and Chatham, primarily on the relatively remote Nauset Beach sandspit.

Orleans

The town is named for Louis-Philippe de Bourbon, Duke of Orleans, who later was the King of France; he supposedly visited this area while exiled during the French Revolution. In the War of 1812 residents claimed to have driven off attacking British ships.

Major industries in the late 1800s were commercial fishing, shipbuilding, and saltmaking. Today, Orleans offers a variety of restaurants, lodging facilities, shops, and travel-related services with ready access to the National Seashore.

The **Nauset (Orleans) Beach** is within the National Seashore but is town-owned and operated; fees are charged in spring and summer. A surfing area is provided.

Boating opportunities abound with 20 town landings providing access to Cape Cod Bay and to Pleasant Bay, which in turn leads to the Atlantic and Nantucket Sound. Several boatyards offer boat and equipment rentals.

Other places of interest: Orleans Historical Society, French Cable Station Museum, Jonathan Young Windmill.

Brewster

The town of Brewster is on the sheltered Cape Cod Bay side of the upper arm where the trees grow taller and the grass thicker than they do between Eastham and Provincetown. Old ship captains' houses and giant elms line Mass. 6A, which meanders through town. Numerous antiques shops, restaurants, and other travel facilities also line the highway.

The **Cape Cod Museum of Natural History**, a nonprofit organization on Mass. 6A, preserves in conjunction with a town-owned reserve an ancient herring run between Cape Cod Bay and freshwater ponds. The museum, open year round, offers ecology exhibits, nature trails, films, lectures, and, in the spring, opportunities to watch alewives run on Stony Brook. For further information, write: P.O. Box 1710, Brewster, MA 02631-0016; telephone 508-896-3867.

At **Stony Brook Mill**, on Stony Brook Road off Mass. 6A, you can see corn ground at a water-powered gristmill and tour a miller's museum.

The **Brewster Historical Society Museum**, on Mass. 6A in East Brewster, exhibits local history.

Roland C. Nickerson State Park, on the eastern edge of Brewster, is an excellent place to camp if you plan to spend much time in the National Seashore. The park has 1,955 acres with more than 400 campsites available on a first-come, first-served basis. Recreational activities include freshwater swimming, boating, bicycling, and hiking. For bicyclists the Cape Cod Rail Trail links the state park with the National Seashore 8 miles away. For further information, write: Roland C. Nickerson State Park, Main Street, Brewster, MA 02631-0003; telephone 518-896-3491.

For more information about the town, call the Brewster Board of Trade: 508-896-5713.

Chatham

Chatham sits at the Cape's elbow, facing both the Atlantic and Nantucket Sound. As a result, the morning fog seems to stay a little longer in Chatham than elsewhere on the Cape.

Commercial fishing boats still work out of Chatham harbors, but the main activity in the summer is tending to vacationers' needs. Main Street, Mass. 28, is a beehive of shops, motels, and restaurants. The Fourth of July parade and Friday evening summer band concerts are longtime Chatham traditions.

An overlook near the **Coast Guard lighthouse** on Main Street provides excellent views of the Atlantic and of the massive swath cut through the Nauset (North) Beach spit in a storm in 1987.

Just south of the lighthouse, on Morris Island, is the **Monomoy National Wildlife Refuge**, a difficult place to access but a great place for birdwatching.

Guided natural history tours on the island are available through the Cape Cod Museum of Natural History and the Wellfleet Bay Audubon Sanctuary.

Chatham has a few small public beaches and a large one, Harding Beach on Nantucket Sound. Remember, the waters of Nantucket Sound are usually calmer and about 5 degrees warmer than those of the Atlantic.

Diligent history buffs can locate a marker at Stage Harbor commemorating Samuel de Champlain's visit in 1606.

Other places of interest: Old Atwood House, built in 1752, on Stage Harbor Road; Chatham Railroad Museum; Old Gristmill; fishing boats unloading at Chatham Fish Pier.

Brewster house

Jonathan Young Windmill

101

Penniman House

The character of the Cape's landscape changes the farther out you go from the mainland. At Eastham and Wellfleet the land becomes noticeably flatter, the vegetation sparser, and the sand more evident. You've reached the Outer Cape – and the National Seashore.

Eastham is home to the National Seashore's Salt Pond Visitor Center, and Wellfleet is home to its headquarters. A stop at the visitor center east of U.S. 6 is an excellent way to discover – through films, exhibits, publications, interpretive programs, and guided walks – the Outer Cape's many natural and historical features and recreational opportunities (see pages 90-91).

Eastham

When the Pilgrims landed on Cape Cod, a small group led by Myles Standish encountered some Indians on Eastham's bay side. After the Pilgrims had settled in at Plymouth, some of them decided to move back to the Cape, and in 1644 a group founded Nauset, which has been known as Eastham since 1651. One of the Nauset founders, Thomas Prence, governed the whole of Plymouth Colony from Eastham for a few years.

Symbolic of these Plymouth-Eastham ties is the gristmill at **Windmill Park** on the west side of U.S. 6, about 2½ miles past the Orleans border. The mill was built in the 1600s in Plymouth and was reconstructed in Eastham in 1793. The mill is open during the summer and on weekends in the spring and fall (see page 47).

The **Penniman House** on Fort Hill Road is symbolic of another Eastham era: the heyday of sailing ships and whaling. Edward Penniman was 11 years old in 1842 when he left Fort Hill and went to sea. By the time he was 29 he was captain of his own whaler and soon was

Old Schoolhouse Museum

sailing to ports around the world. He returned to Eastham in 1868 to build this ornate house complete with mansard roof, kerosene chandelier, and cupola (see page 49).

The **Nauset Marsh Trail** is a loop that starts and ends at the National Seashore's Salt Pond Visitor Center and goes past its namesake, a former glacial kettle pond that has been inundated by seawater, a salt marsh rich in wildlife, and an abandoned farmstead.

Fort Hill Trail takes a loop through the late-18th century farmstead of Rev. Samuel Treat. You can start at either of 2 parking lots on Fort Hill Road south of the visitor center. It winds past stone walls to Skiff Hill and Fort Hill on the edge of Nauset Marsh and then past the Penniman House. The **Red Maple Swamp Trail** is a spur loop off the Fort Hill Trail.

Other places of interest: whaling, lifesaving items, and other artifacts at the Historical Society's Old Schoolhouse Museum opposite Salt Pond Visitor Center; Doane Rock, a glacial erratic; Coast Guard Beach and Nauset Light Beach; Three Sisters Lighthouses; local historical objects at Swift-Daley House on U.S. 6.

Wellfleet

The town of Wellfleet—which was a part of Eastham and called Billingsgate until 1763—is an old whaling port and still a major fishing and shellfish center on Cape Cod Bay. Some say Wellfleet got its name from being a "whale fleet" base, while others say the name came from the Wallfleet oyster beds area of England.

The center of Wellfleet is small but has several restaurants, shops, art galleries, and other facilities for vacationers. The town boasts of its First Congregational Church clock that strikes ship's time.

The Massachusetts Audubon Society runs the 700-acre **Wellfleet Bay Wildlife Sanctuary** west of U.S. 6 in South Wellfleet. Trails go through beach, marsh, and pine forest. It's a good place for birdwatching.

Past the sanctuary, to the east of U.S. 6, is the **National Seashore headquarters**. Informational services are provided here when the Province Lands Visitor Center is closed in the winter.

The **Marconi Station Site**, located past the headquarters on a bluff facing the Atlantic, is where Guglielmo Marconi transmitted the first transatlan-

Wellfleet church door

tic radio message, between Theodore Roosevelt and the King of England, in January 1903 (see pages 78-79).

While you're at the Marconi Station Site, take the 1.2-mile **Atlantic White Cedar Swamp Trail** (see page 97).

On Wellfleet's west side, another trail leads out to and across **Great Island**, a glacial remnant that has become a peninsula. This former island was once dotted with lookout towers for whales and was the location of houses and a tavern.

Other places of interest: Atwood-Higgins House (inquire at National Seashore visitor centers); Wellfleet Historical Society museum on Main Street; Marconi Beach.

Trail to Great Island

The narrowing of the Outer Cape and the power of nature readily become evident in Truro and Provincetown. Here the way the wind and the sea move sand around seems to be more noticeable than elsewhere on the peninsula.

Even in the summer, Truro is relatively desolate for a Cape Cod town, especially when compared with its bustling neighbor to the north, Provincetown, with its writers, artists, actors, and tourists.

Truro rowboats

Truro

Many towns claim many associations with the Pilgrims, and Truro can certainly claim its own. Myles Standish and a small *Mayflower* group discovered a basket of corn that had been buried by Indians on what is now known as Corn Hill, and another group found a freshwater spring near Pilgrim Lake (see pages 34-35).

The town, originally called Pamet and then Dangerfield, took the name of Truro in 1709 because of its similarities to an area of seaside moors and valleys by that name in England.

Whaling ships once worked out of Pamet Harbor on Cape Cod Bay, and until the 1860s the town was a major port with its related shipbuilding and fishing facilities and its saltworks. Most of the men made their living at sea, and in 1841 the town lost 57 fishermen in one storm. Today the small center of town has a few restaurants and other facilities for travelers.

Highland Light—also known as Cape Cod Light—is the second lighthouse constructed on the high bluff overlooking the Atlantic at Truro. The first was built in 1797 and the present one in 1857. Today the U.S. Coast Guard also maintains a radio beacon here to assist ships in their navigation. Nearby is the Truro Historical Society's **Highland House Museum**.

The National Seashore has two short trails in the Pilgrim Heights area of North Truro. **Pilgrim Spring Trail** takes you through the area where a *Mayflower* exploratory group supposedly found a freshwater spring. **Small's Swamp Trail** loops through a farmstead that was abandoned in 1922; the Small family built their house in a glacial kettle hole.

Other points of interest: Pamet Cranberry Bog house; a Paul Revere bell in the 1827 Bell Church on Meetinghouse Road; Head of the Meadow Beach.

Provincetown

The town has been a prominent port and fishing community since colonial days when wharves lined the shores and hundreds of sailing ships filled the harbor. Today Provincetown is still a major port, but cod, mackerel, and hake have long since replaced whales as the major catch. And today, the town is full of art galleries, theaters, sidewalk cafes, restaurants, and shops that come alive in the summer when the population jumps from about 3,000 to 30,000.

Symbolic of Provincetown's long history connected with the sea is the town's Blessing of the Fleet festival on the last weekend in June. In the harbor, colorfully decorated fishing boats pass before a Roman Catholic bishop to receive his blessing for a successful season, and paraders wander through the narrow streets to honor Saint Peter, the patron saint of fishermen.

Whereas the center of town is located on the Cape Cod Bay side of the Cape, another center of interest, **Race Point**, is on the Atlantic side. The National Seashore's Province Lands Visitor Center on Race Point Road has exhibits and

Highland Light

films about the area's natural and human history and is the starting point for a bicycle trail (see page 96). The center offers a variety of guided walks and talks and, from the observation deck, views over the dunes of the ocean—and possibly of whales.

In the summer, the **Old Harbor Life Saving Museum** at Race Point Beach presents interpretive talks and displays about the Cape's early lifesaving activities. The station, on the National Register of Historic Places, was moved to Race Point from Chatham in 1978.

For swimming and sunbathing, the National Park Service manages beaches at Race Point and Herring Cove.

Back in town, the **Pilgrim Monument** rises 255 feet, a prominent reminder that the Pilgrims landed here before heading to Plymouth. Climb to the top of this granite tower

and you are rewarded with wonderful views of the Atlantic and of Cape Cod Bay with the Manomet bluffs near Plymouth on the horizon. The ground-level museum houses memorabilia of the town.

The **Provincetown Heritage Museum** at 356 Commercial Street has a number of maritime paintings, a half-size model of the schooner *Rose Dorothea*, the fishing boat *Charlotte*, and other memorabilia.

Other points of interest: the Seth Nickerson House, circa 1746, at 72 Commercial Street; Provincetown Art Association and Museum; Center for Coastal Studies; whale-watching excursions starting at the MacMillan Wharf.

Old Harbor Life Saving Museum, Provincetown

Blessing of the fleet, Provincetown

Mayflower *replica, Plymouth*

The historical, cultural, recreational, and scenic attractions of Cape Cod and the nearby area are so multitudinous they cannot be listed in this book. Here, by community, are a few sites related thematically to the National Seashore.

Bourne

The 7-mile-long Cape Cod Canal links Massachusetts Bay with Buzzards Bay and saves mariners 100 miles of traveling around the Cape in hazardous waters. The Army Corps of Engineers manages the canal and the 3 bridges that cross it. The canal was first envisioned by Myles Standish in 1624, and 150 years later George Washington liked the idea so much he ordered a survey. But nothing happened for years. New York financier August Belmont took over the construction in 1909 after it had been worked on for nearly 30 years. He saw it through to completion in 1914, but he lost millions of dollars on it. The Federal Government took over the canal in 1928, and the Army Corps deepened and widened it. Stop at the canal visitor center on Main Street in Bourne Monday through Friday to see a model of the canal and an

audiovisual show. Canal boat tours are offered out of Onset Bay Town Pier. Hikers and bicyclists can take a 14-mile roundtrip along the canal.

Woods Hole

The National Marine Fisheries Service Aquarium has tanks of seals, East Coast fish and shellfish, and exhibits about fisheries. The Marine Biological Laboratory offers a tour in the summer of a lab and of sea life in holding tanks. It also presents a slide show about its scientific studies.

Mashpee

The Wampanoag Indian Museum on Mass. 130 has exhibits and artifacts of early Wampanoag life (see pages 32-33).

Plymouth

In this Massachusetts Bay town you can see Plymouth Rock, the traditional landing spot of the Pilgrims after they left Cape Cod in 1620; go aboard a replica of the *Mayflower*; tour Plimoth Plantation, a reconstruction of the Pilgrims' first village; and see a number of other historic sites, plus Cranberry World Visitor Center's exhibits on the cultivation and harvesting of cranberries.

New Bedford

Nantucket and New Bedford were the centers of New England's whaling industry in the 19th century. Today New Bedford is still a key fishing port, but whaling is an historical attraction. The New Bedford Whaling Museum on Johnny Cake Hill features the 89-foot *Lagoda*, a half-scale model of a fully rigged whaling ship; a large collection of scrimshaw; and a multitude of whaling artifacts. Nearby is the Seaman's Bethel, a sailors' church with a pulpit in the shape of a ship's prow. The church figured in Herman Melville's *Moby Dick*.

Awashonks *figurehead, New Bedford Whaling Museum*

While visiting Cape Cod, consider spending a day or two or more on the islands of Martha's Vineyard and Nantucket, summertime havens that share much of the Cape's cultural history and scenic ambience. Both islands were settled in the 1600s by colonists from the Massachusetts Bay Colony, both were major seaports linked with Cape fisheries, and both have attracted vacationers since the steamboat days of the 1800s. Despite these similarities, the islands are distinctive.

Martha's Vineyard is closest – only 7 miles and 45 minutes by ferry from Woods Hole. Nantucket is about 30 miles from the Cape and 2 hours and 20 minutes by ferry from Hyannis. And don't feel you have to take your car. Bicycles, mopeds, taxis, and buses are available.

Martha's Vineyard

New England's largest island, Martha's Vineyard is 24 miles long and 10 miles wide. Vineyard Haven was a major port until the Cape Cod Canal re-routed ship traffic in 1914. Today, the ferry stops at Vineyard Haven and, in the summer, at Oak Bluffs, an old Methodist camp meeting site.

The Vineyard's eclectic architecture includes Victorian gingerbread houses and cottages in Oak Bluffs, sturdy white clapboard sea captains' houses in Edgartown, a mix of styles in Vineyard Haven, fishing shanties in Menemsha, and cedar-shingled cottages throughout the island.

Examine whaling artifacts at the Dukes County Historical Museum in Edgartown, look for ospreys at the Felix Neck Wildlife Sanctuary, inspect solar- and wind-powered energy sources at the Windfarm Museum, and visit Gay Head's scenic cliffs overlooking the Atlantic.

Nantucket

Nantucket is the name not only of the island but of the county and of the main town on the island, which is 14 miles long and 3½ miles wide. The island is known for its more than 800 houses built between 1740 and 1840, for its brick sidewalks and cobblestone streets, for its encircling 55 miles of beautiful beaches, and for its whaling and Quaker heritage.

Nantucket's architecture reflects the great wealth garnered by its whaling merchants and captains. The most notable structures are the Three Bricks and the Two Greeks, mansions built across from each other by Joseph Starbuck and William Hadwen respectively.

Be sure to see the old whaleboat and other seafaring artifacts at the Whaling Museum; ship captain portraits, old baskets, and other historical

Osprey

objects at the Peter Foulger Museum; the elegant ballroom in the William Hadwen House. These sites are administered by the Nantucket Historical Association (508-228-1894). You may also visit a re-created beach station at the Nantucket Life Saving Museum. And don't be startled if you hear Nantucketers refer to the mainland as America. It's a sign of their isolation and independence.

Information

Martha's Vineyard Chamber of Commerce, P.O. Box 1698, Beach Road, Vineyard Haven, MA 02568-1698; 508-693-0085. Nantucket Visitor Services, 25 Federal St., Nantucket, MA 02554-3573; 508-228-0925.

Main Street, Nantucket

Most of the regulations enforced within the National Seashore concern the protection of natural and cultural resources. Others deal with personal safety. Please obey them.

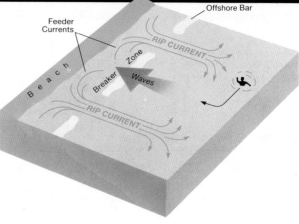

● State law requires the wearing of seatbelts by drivers and passengers in Massachusetts.

● Do not disturb or damage any natural features, including flowers, trees, animals, dunes, marine animal remains, or cultural features, such as historic structures and objects. It is permissible to collect shells, but metal detectors are not allowed.

● Keep beaches, trails, roadsides, and other areas clean. Put all litter in trash receptacles or carry it away with you.

● Motorized vehicles, including mopeds, are not allowed on paved bicycle trails. Over-sand vehicles must be used only on designated sand routes, and a permit—which may be obtained at the Race Point Ranger Station—is required. Indiscriminate off-road driving is prohibited.

● At the ocean, be alert for underwater obstacles. Keep children within reach. Be wary of too much sun exposure. Glass containers, rafts, rubber tubes, snorkels, and masks are not permitted on lifeguarded beaches. Public nudity is prohibited within the National Seashore.

● Kite flying is prohibited within 500 feet of posted shorebird nesting areas.

Rip currents, often incorrectly called rip tides, occur when wave-driven currents surge back to sea through gaps in an offshore bar, then dissipate quickly in deeper water. To escape a rip current, swim parallel to shore before heading in. Never swim against a rip current!

● Keep pets under physical restraint at all times. Leashes must not exceed 6 feet. Pets are not allowed in public buildings, in picnic areas, on lifeguarded beaches, on nature trails, in posted shorebird nesting areas, and on beaches or in water of freshwater ponds.

● At ponds gasoline-powered motorboats, glass containers, and any use of soaps and detergents are prohibited.

● Open fires are not allowed except when authorized by a permit, which can be obtained at visitor centers. Permits are not required for stoves using manufactured fuels, or for charcoal grills when they are used in designated picnic areas at Beech Forest, Pilgrim Heights, Great Island, and Doane Rock, or on sandy or rock beaches bordering tidewater.

● Avoid walking in sand dunes so as not to affect the fragile vegetation. Because sand collapses easily, do not climb cliffs and sandy slopes or dig deep holes in the sand.

● Be alert for ticks. A bite may transmit various ailments. The deer tick is known to

Deer tick magnified
carry Lyme disease. Inspect yourself carefully if you walk through grass or brush.

● Upland game and migratory waterfowl may be hunted in certain National Seashore areas in specified seasons. Federal, state, and local laws apply. Ask for information on hunting opportunities and regulations.

Note: Rangers can provide first aid assistance. The closest health clinics are in Provincetown, Wellfleet, and Harwich, and the nearest hospital is in Hyannis.

CAPE COD
National
Seashore

Eastern National Park & Monument Association, a nonprofit group that supports interpretive and scientific efforts at Cape Cod National Seashore, offers books, maps, and other Cape Cod items for sale at the park and by mail. For a free list of Cape Cod publications, including a special selection for children, write to the association at Salt Pond Visitor Center, Rt. 6, Eastham, MA 02642-2113. For a list of official handbooks about other national parks, write to the Division of Publications, National Park Service, P.O. Box 50, Harpers Ferry, WV 25425-0050.

Here is a partial list of books and booklets about Cape Cod and related subjects:

O'Brien, Greg, editor. *A Guide to Nature on Cape Cod and the Islands.* Written in cooperation with Cape Cod Museum of Natural History. Penguin Books, 1990.

Beston, Henry. *Outermost House.* Holt, Rinehart and Winston, 1928. Reprint First Owl Book Edition, 1992.

Burling, Francis P. *The Birth of Cape Cod National Seashore.* The Leyden Press, 1979.

Clark, Admont G. *Lighthouses of Cape Cod, Martha's Vineyard and Nantucket: Their History and Lore.* Parnassus Imprints, 1992.

Coulombe, Deborah A. *Seaside Naturalist: A Guide to Nature Study at the Seashore.* Prentice-Hall, 1984.

Dalton, J.W. *The Life Savers of Cape Cod.* Barta Press, 1902. Reprint Parnassus Imprints, 1991.

Finch, Robert. *Common Ground: A Naturalist's Cape Cod.* David R. Godine, 1981; *Outlands: Journeys to the Outer Edges of Cape Cod.* David R. Godine, 1986; *The Primal Place.* W.W. Norton, 1983.

Hay, John. *The Great Beach.* Doubleday, 1963.

Kaye, Glen. *Cape Cod: the Story Behind the Scenery.* KC Publications, 1980.

Kittredge, Henry C. *Cape Cod: Its People and Their History.* Houghton Mifflin, 1930. Reprint Parnassus Imprints, 1987.

Martin, Kenneth. *Some Very Handsome Work.* Eastern National Park and Monument Association, 1991.

Oldale, Robert. *Cape Cod and the Islands: The Geologic Story.* Parnassus Imprints, 1992.

Penniman, Augusta. *Penniman Journal: A Whaling Voyage.* Eastern National Park & Monument Association, 1988.

Quinn, William P. *Shipwrecks Around Cape Cod.* Lower Cape Publishing, 1973.

Teal, John and Mildred. *Life and Death of the Salt Marsh.* 1969. Reprint Ballantine Books, 1991.

Thoreau, Henry David. *Cape Cod.* Houghton Mifflin, 1864, and Penguin State, 1865. Reprint Parnassus Imprints with introduction by Robert Finch, 1984. Reprint Penguin Books with introduction by Paul Theroux, 1987.

Waldron, Nan Turner. *Journey to Outermost House.* Butterfly & Wheel Publishing, 1991.

Weinstein-Farson, Laurie. *The Wampanoag.* Chelsea House, 1989.

Willison, George F. *Saints and Strangers.* Reynal & Hitchcock, 1945. Reprint Parnassus Imprints, 1983.

Index

Library of Congress Cataloging-in-Publication Data
Finch, Robert, 1943-
Cape Cod : its natural and cultural history : a Guide to Cape Cod National Seashore. Massachusetts / by Robert Finch; produced by the Division of Publications, National Park Service, U.S. Department of the Interior.
p.   cm.—(Official National Park handbook, Cape Cod National Seashore; handbook 148)
Includes index.
1. Cape Cod National Seashore (Mass.)—Guidebooks. I. United States. National Park Service. Division of Publications. II. Title. III. Series: Handbook (United States. National Park Service. Division of Publications); 148.
F72.C3F55 1993 917.44'920443 —dc20 92-40414 CIP Supt. of Docs. no.: I 29.9/5: 148
ISBN 0-912627-56-5

☆ GPO:1997—417-646/40503
Printed on recycled paper
Reprint 1997

Sharp-tailed sparrow

National Park Service

The National Park Service expresses its appreciation to all those persons who made the preparation and production of this handbook possible. The Service especially thanks Eastern National Park and Monument Association and The Friends of Cape Cod National Seashore for their financial support of this publication. All photos and artwork not credited below come from the files of Cape Cod National Seashore. Some materials are restricted against commercial reproduction. The book was designed by Richard Sheaff.

John Arsenault 95 whale watchers
Frank Balthis, 106 *Mayflower*
Tony Bonanno 62-63 Nauset C.G. Station, 104 rowboats
Tom Cawley, 43 sea-lavender and terrapin, 66-67 snowy egret, ruddy turnstone, and willet, 82-83 nightshade, heather, beach plum, cactus, dewberry, St. Johnswort, bell-flower, mayflower, aster, laurel, star-flower, and cypress spurge
Concord Free Public Library 73 Thoreau
Donald Demers 38-39 Atwood-Higgins art, mortise
R.R. Donnelley GeoSystems 87 map, 88-89
Steve Dunwell back cover, 17, 19, 22, 68, 90 girl, 93 fisher-man, 107 Nantucket
Roger Everett 66-67 dunin, spotted sandpiper, merganser, yellowlegs, canvasback, eider, green-backed heron, sanderlings
Jeff Gnass 47, 102 schoolhouse, 105 station
Laurel Guadazno 82 goldenrod
Vincent Guadazno 59
William Hartley 16, 42-43 salt hay, snail, sea stars, scallop, lobster, anemone, eelgrass, sea robin, hermit, jelly, rock crabs, sea lettuce, 44, 66 osprey and oystercatcher, 82 water lily
Steven Heaslip, Cape Cod Times 28 inset
Historical Society of Old Yarmouth 51 Eldridge
William Johnson 6, 30, 53, 84-85, 86 umbrella, 92 lifeguard, 96 bikers, 101 windmill, 102 Penniman, 103 Great Island, 104 lighthouse, 109
Library of Congress, 32 Debry, 33 Champlain map, 36 both
Brad Luther, Coastal News Publications 60 map
Ralph MacKenzie 2-3, 9, 13, 18, 67 common terns and great blue heron, 87 artist, 100, 101 house, 105 blessing
Mariners Museum, Newport News 51 *Red Jacket*
Linda Minnich 58